MAO ZEDONG

FOUNDER OF THE PEOPLE'S REPUBLIC OF CHINA

BY REBECCA STEFOFF

The Millbrook Press
Brookfield, Connecticut

Photographs courtesy of AP/Wide World: pp. 12, 64, 70, 75, 96; Bettmann: pp. 17, 33, 38, 80, 82, 106, 113; Culver Pictures: pp. 29, 60; Sovfoto/ Eastfoto: pp. 47, 93, 101, 111. Map by Frank Senyk.

Library of Congress Cataloging-in-Publication Data
Stefoff, Rebecca, 1951–
Mao Zedong : founder of the People's Republic of China / by Rebecca Stefoff.
p. cm.
Includes bibliographical references and index.
Summary: A biography of Mao Zedong, founder of a communist state in China in 1949, hailed by some as a hero, by others, a tyrant.
ISBN 1-56294-531-9
1. Mao, Tse-tung, 1893–1976—Juvenile literature. 2. Heads of state—China—Biography—Juvenile literature. 3. China—History—20th century—Juvenile literature. [1. Mao, Tse-tung, 1893–1976. 2. Heads of state. 3. China—History—20th century.]
I. Title
DS778.M3S762 1995
951.05'092—dc20 95-24662 [B] CIP AC

Published by The Millbrook Press, Inc.
2 Old New Milford Road
Brookfield, Connecticut 06804

ABOUT CHINESE SPELLINGS AND NAMES

Chinese writing uses symbols quite unlike those of Western alphabets. The process of making Chinese words readable and pronounceable for Westerners is called romanization, because most Western languages use letters based on the Roman alphabet.

Many systems of romanization have been used over the years to give Chinese names Western spellings. *Pinyin*, the one most commonly used today, was introduced by the Chinese in the 1950s and is now followed by most Western writers. The *pinyin* versions of place-names and personal names are used throughout this book. For example, a large port on China's southern coast is called Guangzhou in *pinyin*, although for many years it was known to non-Chinese people as Canton. China's capital, Beijing, was formerly called both Peiping and Peking. And Mao Zedong used to be known as Mao Tse-tung. Chinese personal names consist of the family name followed by the individual's given name. In the case of Mao Zedong, for example, "Mao" is the family name; in the West it would be considered the "last" name. "Zedong" is the individual name—what Westerners would call the "first" name.

In *pinyin*, the letter *q* at the beginning of a name is pronounced *ch*, as in "church"; *x* is pronounced *sh* as in "show"; *z* is pronounced *ds* as in "reads"; and *zh* is pronounced *j* as in "judge."

C O N T E N T S

MAO ZEDONG

CHAPTER 1

"BRINGER OF THE RED DAWN"

October 1, 1949, dawned cloudy and cold in Beijing, the capital of China. But as a brisk wind blew from the north, the heavy clouds began to clear. By midday the sun was shining fitfully between sudden showers of autumn rain.

Gleams of watery sunlight shone on the roofs of the Forbidden City, a cluster of centuries-old palaces buried deep within the imperial quarter of Beijing. Surrounded by a moat, sealed off from the outside world by a wall more than 2 miles (3 kilometers) long—a wall that was painted a special violet color that only China's emperors could use—the Forbidden City was a symbol of China's imperial glories. Here, in bygone centuries, emperors and empresses had built splendid palaces and temples. Here, silk-clad courtiers had carried out their elaborate intrigues, artists and scholars had presented their finest works, and officials had tended to the business of governing one of the largest empires the world has ever seen.

The wall around the Forbidden City is broken by several gates. One of these is called Tiananmen, the Gate of Heavenly Peace. This gate, 40 feet (12 meters) thick and 100 feet (30 meters) high, was for centuries the chief point of contact between the people of China and their emperors. Imperial pronouncements and new laws were posted at Tiananmen. When China's last emperor, Pu Yi, left his throne in 1912, the end of imperial China was formally proclaimed at Tiananmen. Now, in the autumn of 1949, Tiananmen would be the setting for a new beginning in Chinese history—the establishment of the People's Republic of China under the leadership of Mao Zedong.

The gate had been freshly repainted in the imperial shade of purple, perhaps as a sign that the man who would stand atop Tiananmen on this day was just as powerful as the rulers of old, although he did not call himself emperor. The eaves of the gate were lacquered red and gold. Beneath them large silk banners fluttered in the restless wind. The enormous square before the gate had once been shaded by groves of silk trees, but the trees had been cut down. Now the 98-acre (40-hectare) square was paved with concrete and asphalt. More than a hundred thousand people stood there, waiting for a glimpse of the man who had brought the new China into being.

On the fringes of the crowd, people heard the sound of distant engines coming closer. The parade was approaching. Soon a long row of cars inched past. Onlookers cheered and laughed as one vehicle passed. It was an American-made Sherman tank, which had been sent to China to help crush the People's Liberation Army (PLA), the military arm of the Chinese Communist party (CCP). But the PLA had captured the tank and overcome all opposition, and now the communists were the new masters of China.

The square before Tiananmen was festooned with pennants and slogans in red, the color of international communism. Next to the gate rose a huge portrait of a round-faced, gently smiling man, his black hair brushed back from his broad forehead in two swelling waves. The man in the portrait was Mao Zedong, the chairman of the CCP and the most powerful man in China. Scores of dignitaries were arriving in the parade, but it was Mao whom the people had come to see.

Mao's car followed the tank slowly along the wide street called the Boulevard of Lengthy Peace amid throngs who cried out, "Long live Chairman Mao!" He and the other officials climbed onto the Gate of Heavenly Peace and stood on a balcony 30 feet (9 meters) above the ground, gazing out at the sea of upturned, jubilant faces. Mao stepped forward into the place once reserved for emperors and their heralds. Clad in a simple cloth cap and a gray tunic, the working-class uniform of the Chinese communists, he coughed a little in the cold wind. Then, raising his voice, he announced the birth of a new state, the People's Republic of China. "Thus begins a new

era in the history of China," he declared. "We, the four hundred and seventy-five million people of China, have stood up. We will never be humiliated again. Let the earth tremble."

The ceremony lasted for hours. Each of Mao's comrades on the balcony was introduced and made a speech. Mao and the other high officials of the CCP periodically withdrew into a reception hall to refresh themselves with orange drink, shrimp chips, peanuts, and cigarettes; outside, the spectators bought beer, wine, rice cakes, and other treats from vendors. As the sky darkened into evening, paraders carrying colored lanterns made their way down the crowded boulevard. Drummers and musicians began playing in the square, and people broke into the *yangko*, a peasant dance that celebrated the planting of the rice crop. Beijing's streets were full of revelers, who were giddy with excitement because they had witnessed a momentous turning-point in history. Finally, Mao Zedong appeared one last time on the balcony to shout, "Long live the People's Republic!" and the crowd roared back with a single many-throated voice, "Long live Chairman Mao!"

Mao Zedong announces the birth of the People's Republic of China on October 1, 1949. The Communist victory in China made Mao the most powerful person in the world's most populous nation.

On that day, fifty-five-year-old Mao Zedong achieved the goal of many years: the founding of a communist state in China. In doing so, he fulfilled the hopes of followers who hailed him as "the bringer of the red dawn" and "the red star over China." As a student, a revolutionary, a soldier, and a military commander, Mao had dreamed of bringing change to the world's most populous country. At the head of a peasant army, he had fought a long and bitter battle to sweep out the old order of aristocrats, land-owners, merchants, and foreign powers, who, he believed, had kept the Chinese masses downtrodden and miserable for generations. The road that led him to Beijing and the Gate of Heavenly Peace was a long one, and filled with turmoil. Mao Zedong had been a rebel and a fighter since his earliest days.

Mao Zedong rose to power as the champion of China's rural peasants. He liked to present himself as a humble peasant, identifying himself with the people who, in his view, were the true source of China's strength. He allowed his bodyguards to call him Lao Tu, which means "Old Peasant," and he said, "I am the son of peasants and I have the peasants' living habits."[1]

Although he grew up in the countryside, Mao Zedong did not in fact fit neatly into the peasant class. Zedong was born on December 26, 1893, in the province of Hunan in southern China. His home was in a village called Shaoshan—a name that means "Music Mountain." His father, Mao Shunsheng, came from a poor peasant background but was quite ambitious. Although he could neither read nor write, Mao Shunsheng was a shrewd and practical man who worked hard to make a little money and then used it cleverly to make more money. He set himself up as a trader in rice and pigs; he also made loans to his fellow villagers at high rates of interest. He invested in land, and during Zedong's childhood the Mao family farm grew from 3 to more than 20 acres (1 to 8 hectares). (Many Chinese peasants did not own property but instead worked on land belonging to landowners. Even those peasants who owned land rarely possessed more than 5 acres, or 2 hectares.)

Through Mao Shunsheng's efforts, the Mao family rose to some prominence in Shaoshan. Mao Zedong later admitted to his biographer Edgar Snow that the Maos had been "rich peasants." In fact, they were small landholders who lived better than many of the families around them. Mao Shunsheng employed at least one peasant laborer to work in his fields. This did not mean, however, that life was easy for young Zedong. Like all rural children, he was expected to share the family's tasks, and at the age of six he began working on the farm. His earliest jobs included weeding, frightening birds away from the young rice seedlings, and tending the family's buffalo. As a teenager he worked with the adults to plant and harvest the rice crop. His younger brothers, Zemin and Zetan, shared these chores when they were old enough to work, as did his young adopted sister, Zejian.

When Zedong was eight, his father sent him to the local primary school. Mao Shunsheng wanted the boy to receive some education because a son who knew enough reading, writing, and arithmetic to draw up contracts and keep accounts would be useful to him in his business. But school enlarged Zedong's world in unexpected ways. After he learned to read, he lost himself in books. His favorites were tales of war, banditry, heroic deeds, rebellion, and glory—books with romantic titles like *The Story of the Marshes* and *The Romance of the Three Kingdoms.*

Schoolchildren were not supposed to read these extravagant tales, so Zedong and his classmates hid the forbidden books inside their textbooks whenever the teacher was near. "We learned many of the stories almost by heart," Mao Zedong reminisced years later, "and discussed and rediscussed them many times. We knew more of them than the old men of the village, who also loved them and used to exchange stories with us. I believe that perhaps I was much influenced by such books, read at an impressionable age."[2]

When Mao started school, at the beginning of the twentieth century, Chinese education followed a pattern that had changed little over the centuries. The primary texts were the Chinese classics: the writings of Confucius, a sage who died in 479 B.C., and of the scholars and thinkers who had developed his ideas into a philosophy called Confucianism. Although traditional Chinese culture reflected the influence of

Although no actual portrait survives of Confucius, traditional images show him wearing the robe and cap of an ancient sage. Mao Zedong hated Confucius, who symbolized the rigidity of classical Chinese culture.

many religions—including Buddhism, which came to China from India—Confucianism had formed the basis of Chinese society for two thousand years. The imperial authorities preferred Confucianism because it emphasized such virtues as moderation, order, stability, and respect for authority.

The orderly, authoritarian principles of the Confucian classics did not appeal to the romantic youth who secretly feasted on tales of heroic grandeur. "I hated Confucius from the age of eight," Mao Zedong later said.[3] Like the heroes of his favorite stories, Zedong was a rebel. As time went on, he found himself often at odds with authority, both at home and in school. He was beaten by his father and his teacher, and the beatings fueled his resentment and his sense of injustice.

When Zedong was ten years old, his rebelliousness broke out into open revolt in a confrontation with his teacher. Students who were called upon to recite were expected to follow the proper ritual—to rise, walk to the teacher's desk, face the class, and speak. Zedong thought that such formality was unnecessary. One day when the teacher ordered him to recite, he remained seated on his stool and calmly asked, "If you can hear me well while I sit down, why should I stand up to recite?" The infuriated teacher seized Zedong's collar and pulled the boy up off his stool. Knowing that he was in for another beating, Zedong wriggled out of his teacher's grasp and ran away from the school.

Zedong did not want to go home: His father would be angry with him and would undoubtedly give him a thrashing. He thought of his favorite books. In *The Story of the Marshes*, the rebel heroes fled into the hills. Zedong decided that he would do the same. He spent three days wandering around the countryside outside Shaoshan while the villagers searched for him. At last someone from the Mao household found him and brought him home. "After my return to the family, to my surprise conditions improved somewhat," Mao Zedong later recalled. "My father was slightly more considerate and the teacher was slightly more inclined to moderation. The result of my act of protest impressed me very much. It was a successful 'strike.'"[4] Mao Zedong had learned at an early age that standing up for what he believed in was risky—but it could also win him the respect of others.

Another dramatic confrontation occurred a few years later. Zedong's father had invited guests to the Mao home, and in front of these visitors he began to insult his oldest son, calling Zedong "lazy and useless." Furious and embarrassed, Mao cursed his father. This broke the most basic rule of Confucianism, which demands that children show respect for their fathers. Zedong then ran from the house. His parents ran after him, his mother begging him to restore the household peace and his father cursing him and ordering him to return.

Instead, Zedong ran to the edge of a pond and threatened to jump into it if his father laid hands on him. They argued back and forth in front of the astonished guests and villagers. Mao Shunsheng ordered his son to apologize and perform an elaborate bow of submission. Zedong made a counteroffer: He would perform a small bow, but only if his father promised not to beat him. Finally Mao Shunsheng agreed to these terms. "Thus the war ended," said Mao Zedong, "and from it I learned that when I defended my rights by open rebellion my father relented, but when I remained meek and submissive he only cursed and beat me the more."[5] Once again life seemed to be teaching Zedong that he could improve his situation by courageously defying authority.

Life in the Mao household was strained. Zedong came to hate his father, whom he saw as greedy and overly strict. Zedong and his brother Zemin often conspired with their mother to get their way in spite of Mao Shunsheng. For example, they went behind Mao Shunsheng's back to give food to villagers in need. "My mother was a kind woman, generous and sympathetic, and ever ready to share what she had," said Mao Zedong. "She pitied the poor and often gave them rice when they came to ask for it during famines. But she could not do so when my father was present. He disapproved of charity. We had many quarrels in my home over this question."[6]

There were also quarrels about Zedong's habits and his future. Zedong left primary school at thirteen and took on a full workload for his father, laboring in the fields by day and keeping the account books by night. Yet Zedong's passion for reading was as strong as ever. He tracked down and borrowed every book in Shaoshan village, reading in secret. "I used to cover up the window of my room late at night so that my father would not see the light," he recalled.[7]

Whenever Mao Shunsheng caught Zedong reading, he burst into a torrent of complaints and criticism. Once he found Zedong reading a novel when the boy was supposed to be carrying baskets of manure from the pigsty to the fields. He accused Zedong of being so corrupted by "bad books" that he no longer attended to his duties—only to be struck speechless when Zedong explained that he had already hauled even more manure than he was expected to do. "I will work regularly on the farm, but I want to read my books as well," Zedong insisted, and his father grumblingly gave in.[8]

Mao Shunsheng came up with what he thought was a surefire method of making his rebellious son settle down. He arranged for the thirteen-year-old boy to be married to a twenty-year-old woman. (It was traditional for Chinese parents to arrange their children's marriages.) Zedong objected violently to this scheme. After much argument and many angry words, he agreed to go through with the ceremony, but he refused to live with the woman, and the marriage was soon dissolved.

About this time, while he was smarting from the stings of personal injustice, Zedong witnessed injustice on a larger, social scale. Crop failures brought about a famine in the region. Thousands of people were without food. In Changsha, the capital of Hunan province, hungry crowds protested against the governor in food riots. The imperial officials responded swiftly and harshly. The rioters were branded as insurrectionists, or rebels. They were rounded up and many were beheaded, their heads displayed on poles as a warning to others.

Zedong and other young men of Shaoshan discussed the food riots and the governor's treatment of the rebels for days. "It made a deep impression on me," he later told an interviewer. "Most of the other students sympathized with the 'insurrectionists,' but only from an observer's point of view. They did not understand that it had any relation to their own lives. They were merely interested in it as an exciting incident. I never forgot it. I felt that there with the rebels were ordinary people like my own family and I deeply resented the injustice of the treatment given to them."[9] Mao Zedong had begun to take an interest in events in the wider world outside Shaoshan, and he sensed that there were connections between his own life and those events.

Throughout Zedong's childhood, the village of Shaoshan had seemed a quiet, peaceful oasis, far from the rest of the world. There were no newspapers; news reached Shaoshan slowly, after many months or even years. The villagers lived as their ancestors had, in an unchanging world of silver water, green rice shoots, and fog-shrouded mountain peaks.

Yet all the while, change was brewing in the world outside Shaoshan, and hints of that change began to ruffle the smooth surface of village life. In his eagerness to read everything that he could get his hands on, Zedong came across a pamphlet that told how the once-mighty Chinese empire was losing territory and power to Japan and other nations. The pamphlet began with words that were to haunt Zedong for decades: "Alas, China will be subjugated." Later he said, "After I read this I felt depressed about the future of my country and began to realize that it was the duty of all people to help save it."[10]

Another book, called *Words of Warning*, described modern industrial developments such as the telephone, telegraph, railway, and steamship and told how they could benefit China. These ideas excited Zedong and made him curious about the world beyond his village. "May you live in interesting times" is an old Chinese curse. It is meant to be a wish of ill fortune, because the times that the historians find most interesting are often quite uncomfortable for the people who live through them. As he stood on the threshold of Shaoshan, eagerly absorbing news from the outside world, the teenage Mao Zedong began to realize that he lived in very interesting times indeed.

TURMOIL IN
2 AN ANCIENT LAND

China is home to one of the world's oldest cultures. As long ago as 4000 B.C., settled farming communities existed along the Huang River in north-central China, the region that was the birthplace of Chinese civilization. By the eighteenth century B.C., a royal family called the Shang dynasty had gained control of the Huang Valley, creating the first organized Chinese state. Another dynasty, the Zhou, came to power in the same region in 1122 and 1027 B.C. Literature and the arts flourished under the Zhou, and two of China's most celebrated thinkers, Lao-tzu and Confucius, produced the philosophical writings that became the cornerstones of classical Chinese culture.

For centuries, rival dynasties rose and fell in various parts of China. Warring states vied for power. Then, in 221 B.C., Shi Huangdi, a prince of the Qin dynasty, conquered these warring states and became the first ruler of a united Chinese empire—the largest empire on earth, with 40 million subjects. Shi Huangdi also began building the Great Wall to protect the Chinese heartland from the nomadic invaders who occasionally swarmed into China from the north.

The Qin dynasty was succeeded by the Han dynasty (206 B.C.–A.D. 220). Under the Han emperors, Buddhism was introduced to China and later developed into a major Chinese religion. Parts of Korea, Southeast Asia, and Central Asia were added to the Chinese empire. The Han era was followed by several centuries of warfare, during which China was wracked by internal strife and was also invaded by tribespeople from the north and west. The empire was reunited under the Sui dynasty (581–618) and strengthened under the Tang dynasty (618–907). Crafts, arts, and trade advanced under the Tang rulers. Many important scientific advances were made under their successors, the Song emperors, who ruled China from 960 until 1279. During the Song era, the Chinese invented gunpowder, movable type, and the magnetic compass, long before these were developed in the West.

The Song dynasty collapsed when Mongols from the north, led by Genghis Khan and Khublai Khan, invaded and conquered China. The Mongols founded a new dynasty, the Yuan, which ruled China until the late fourteenth century. Under the Mongols, China received its first official emissaries from Europe—

notably Marco Polo, the Italian traveler whose tale of his long stay in Khublai's court fascinated European readers for generations. In 1368 the Chinese overthrew the Yuan dynasty and replaced it with the Ming, a native Chinese ruling family. The Ming emperors remained in control of China until 1644. They wanted Chinese culture and politics to remain free of foreign influences, so they established a policy of isolation from the rest of the world that kept China's borders closed for centuries. Very few Chinese were permitted to leave their homeland, and foreigners were allowed only the most limited contact with China. A few European nations were able to establish trading posts in certain ports, but Europeans were strictly forbidden to travel within China.

In 1644, China was once again invaded from the north. Warriors from Manchuria (now the northeastern part of China) conquered the Chinese empire and established their own dynasty, the Qing. The Manchu, or Qing, emperors continued the Ming policy of keeping China isolated from the rest of the world. They also added Tibet, Manchuria, Mongolia, and much of Central Asia to the empire.

On the surface, the history of the Chinese empire from the distant past through the Qing dynasty seems to be one of change and turbulence. Periods of firm central rule under powerful dynasties or exceptionally capable emperors alternated with eras of internal conflict or disruption when no strong leader emerged to hold the empire together. Dynasties rose and fell, and several of them—notably the Yuan and the Qing—were founded by invaders from outside China who came to conquer and remained to rule. Surprisingly, however, the language, art, and culture of China changed hardly at all over thousands of years.

China's culture remained stable partly because the country was isolated from other major centers of civilization. Some of this isolation was geographic. China was separated from India and the Mediterranean region by deserts and mountain ranges. Overland journeys along trade routes, such as the fabled Silk Road, were formidable undertakings, and the sea routes linking China to other civilizations were also perilous. But the isolation was also self-imposed. China's leaders regarded China as the only true civilization, the center of the world—the Middle Kingdom, as the Chinese called their homeland. The people of all other nations were seen as barbarians, incapable of offering anything worthwhile or interesting to the Chinese.

But there was another reason for China's long-lasting cultural stability. Things did not change much in China because unchangingness was built into Chinese tradition. The values most emphasized in classical Chinese culture included harmony, obedience, and respect for order and authority—qualities that reinforced social stability and discouraged change. In addition, the imperial government was a powerful force against change. Emperors and even dynasties changed with the passing years, but the enormous, complex bureaucracy that had evolved to govern the empire in the emperor's name kept life moving in its accustomed course.

By the nineteenth century, however, the calm, ordered surface of Chinese life was beginning to crack. Foreigners were knocking ever more insistently at China's gates. European and American merchants, eager to sell their goods to millions of new customers, demanded that China admit foreign traders. Western governments, listening to the demands of the merchants, put pressure on the empire.

Great Britain began selling opium from its India colony to dealers in China, despite strict Chinese laws against the sale of the drug. Soon opium addiction was such a serious problem that the Manchu rulers passed harsh new laws against foreign goods and traders. The British responded with force, and the result was the First Opium War (1839–1842). Unable to compete with British gunboats and artillery, the Chinese were defeated and compelled to open more ports to Western ships. The Second Opium War (1856–1860) pitted China against Great Britain and France. Once again, China was defeated and humiliated. The Chinese were forced to grant the Western nations considerable control over China's territory and commerce.

While China suffered ever-increasing interference from foreign governments, the country was also undergoing internal convulsions. China's population was growing, but the amount of farmland was not. As a

British troops capture a Chinese city in the First
Opium War, 1839-1842. The two Opium Wars
fueled China's resentment of foreign domination.

result, it was harder each year for China to feed its people. A year or two of crop failures could bring disaster to millions of the poorest Chinese. And in the mid-nineteenth century, disaster struck. A series of floods and crop failures resulted in widespread food shortages. Famine was severe in parts of southern China, a region that was also plagued by banditry and lawlessness. Rebellion against Manchu rule broke out again and again in the south when dissatisfied peasants rose up against the imperial government.

Most of these peasant rebellions were small and easily crushed by imperial troops. But an uprising that began in 1851 turned into the bloodiest civil war the world has ever seen. It was called the Taiping Rebellion, and it was led by a peasant named Hung Hsui-ch'uan, who claimed to have had religious visions that inspired him to preach the "Tai-ping Tien-kuo" (Heavenly Dynasty of Perfect Peace). He mustered an ill-equipped but enormous peasant army that devastated much of China for a decade and a half in its attempts to overthrow the Qing dynasty. Eventually British troops stepped in to help the Manchus put down the Taipings—another piece of foreign interference that fueled the resentment many Chinese felt toward Westerners.

The Taiping Rebellion ended in 1864 when its leader committed suicide. It had cost 20 million lives. Although the uprising ended in defeat for the rebellious peasants, it left a legacy for later revolutionaries, including Mao Zedong. The Taipings proved that China's poor peasants could form a powerful army, capable of challenging imperial troops and even of winning major battles. Mao learned this lesson well. Later he was to claim that any revolution in China must start with the peasants. And the Taiping rebels, who wanted not only to challenge authority but to establish a whole new social order, were forerunners of the idealists who followed Mao's revolutionary banner.

By the late nineteenth century, China's imperial dynasty had become weak. Russia, Japan, Great Britain, France, the United States, and Germany carved out sections of Chinese territory to administer. These countries also had a hand in managing China's finances, railroads, and trade. Many Chinese were disgusted with this state of affairs. Their fears about the future of their country were reflected in the dismal prophecy that so alarmed the young Mao Zedong: "Alas, China will be subjugated." More and more Chinese started to feel that it was time to kick the foreigners out.

Nationalism—the feeling that China's destiny should be controlled by the will of the Chinese people—was on the rise. Nationalist societies formed to protest the presence of foreigners in China. One such group was the Society of the Righteous Harmonious Fists, nicknamed the Boxers because its members practiced a martial art. In 1899 the Boxers organized an uprising, hoping to drive all non-Chinese out of the country. They killed many foreigners and imprisoned others in the embassy quarter of Beijing.

The Boxer Rebellion was short-lived and unsuccessful. It ended when a force of Japanese, German, Russian, American, French, and British troops smashed the uprising. The spirit of Chinese nationalism, however, was by no means dead. Indeed, nationalism grew stronger—and the Qing dynasty weaker—in the years after the Boxer Rebellion.

Impatience with the Manchus and with foreign meddling was not the only reason for unrest in China as the nineteenth century drew to an end and the twentieth century began. There was also rising discontent with the social order that for generations had kept landlords rich and peasants poor. Spurred by hard times, the poor and landless masses began organizing and calling for change, just as the Taipings had done a few decades earlier. One of their organizations, the Elder Brother Society, had members all over southern China.

Many men in and around Shaoshan, Mao Zedong's home village, belonged to the Society. In an attempt at revolt that deeply impressed the teenage Mao, these men disputed their rent payments to a local landlord. The landlord sued them and won the case after bribing the judge. Led by a blacksmith named Pang, the Elder Brothers rioted against the landlord and the local government. They retreated to a mountain hideout but were flushed out by imperial troops. Pang was beheaded. "In the eyes of the students, however, he was a hero," said Mao Zedong later, "for all sympathized with the revolt."[1]

Boxer fighters in prison after their capture by foreign troops. The crushing of the Boxer Rebellion did not quell Chinese nationalism, which continued to gain strength.

Revolt struck even closer to Mao's home a year later. Afflicted by a food shortage, peasants demanded that the rich landowners open their storerooms and give free rice to the poor. Mao Zedong's father, Mao Shunsheng, had accumulated a store of rice and was selling it to merchants in Changsha. One of Mao Shunsheng's rice shipments was seized by the peasants. Mao Zedong later recalled how his father reacted: "His wrath was boundless. I did not sympathize with him. At the same time I thought the villagers' method was wrong also."[2] The young Mao Zedong was moved by the peasants' suffering and by their desire for fairer treatment, yet he was troubled by the violence and lawlessness of their actions. In later years, though, he would come to believe that violence was a necessary part of reform.

By the time Mao Zedong reached the age of sixteen, he had seen his peaceful village touched by revolt. He knew that China had been humiliated by foreign powers and that the Manchu government was weak and decayed. The China in which he was growing to manhood was a land in which ancient ways were breaking down, and new ideas were in the air. Mao Zedong felt the stirrings of political purpose. He knew that something important was happening in China, and he wanted to be part of it. The first step was to get out of Shaoshan.

CHAPTER 3

YOUNG REVOLUTIONARY

Mao Zedong's greatest desire was to study at one of the "modern" schools that had begun to appear in some Chinese cities. Modeled after the schools run by foreign missionaries, these modern schools taught such subjects as history, science, mathematics, and world geography as well as the Chinese classics. But Mao Shunsheng sneered at his son's request to continue his education.

Quietly and persistently, Mao Zedong went to work. He spoke to his mother's relatives and to friends of the Mao family, borrowing a bit of money from each. Finally Zedong faced his father at dinner one night and announced that he intended to study at the East Mountain Higher Primary School in the town of Xiang Xiang, 15 miles (24 kilometers) away. "Perhaps you have won a lottery ticket this morning and have suddenly become rich?" said Mao

Shunsheng scornfully. With that, Zedong displayed the money he had painstakingly saved. He even agreed to hire a laborer to take over his chores on the farm. Mao Shunsheng was left with nothing to say. At dawn the next day Mao Zedong walked out of Shaoshan village with a bundle of possessions: two old and patched sheets, two shirts, and a few books.

Once he had entered the black lacquered gates of the East Mountain School in September 1909, Mao Zedong found himself the object of taunts and teasing. He was much taller and four or five years older than the other boys, and his patched clothes and rural accent marked him as an outsider among the well-to-do boys of the city. But the headmaster was sufficiently impressed with Mao's earnest manner to admit him to the school.

Mao made few friends at East Mountain, but he worked hard at his studies. He dove eagerly into the study of world history and was entranced by the forcefulness of military heroes like Napoleon Bonaparte, George Washington, and Peter the Great of Russia. Often he quoted to his schoolmates sentences that had impressed him. One such sentence was about George Washington: "Victory and independence only came to the U.S.A. after eight long bitter years of fighting under Washington."[1]

Mao was fascinated by the American and French revolutions; he wondered whether revolution was possible in China. On one point he remained stubborn, to the amusement of his classmates and the vexation of his teachers. He insisted that the stories in *The Romance of the Three Kingdoms* and his other beloved novels were true. Once he went so far as to throw a chair at a student who said that the novels were merely fictional tales.

By September 1911, Mao felt that he had learned all that he could at East Mountain. He was impatient to see something of the larger world, and with the help of one of his East Mountain teachers he was admitted to a secondary school in the provincial capital, Changsha. He scraped together enough money to travel to Changsha as a third-class passenger on a river steamer. With about 800,000 people, Changsha was the biggest and most exciting place Mao had ever seen. Each day brought new sights and adventures. He saw his first newspaper in Changsha—and within a matter of weeks he had written his first published article, which appeared in a nationalist paper called *Strength of the People.*

Mao spent only four weeks in school. Like thousands of other Chinese young people, he was caught up in the events that were sweeping through China. The nationalist movement had gained force and form under the leadership of Sun Yatsen, a physician who had emerged as one of the principal opponents of the Manchu dynasty. Now some of the nationalists launched a revolution in Hunan province, calling for the end of Manchu rule and the establishment of a Chinese republic. A member of the republican forces came to Mao's school and stirred up the students

Educated in Hawaii and Hong Kong, Sun Yatsen had many ties to the West. He won support from outside China for his struggle to overthrow the Manchu dynasty.

with talk of the new era that was dawning. Fired with enthusiasm, Mao left school and enlisted in the Hunan revolutionary army.

Mao lived in an army garrison in Changsha. The army paid him seven dollars a month; he spent two on food and water and the rest on newspapers. He ran errands for the officers and wrote letters for his fellow soldiers, who were illiterate. After six or seven months, during which Mao did no fighting, much of southern China was in the hands of the republicans. Sun Yatsen and a Manchu general named Yuan Shikai signed a truce that forced Pu Yi, the last Qing emperor, to step down from the throne. The Republic of China was proclaimed in 1912 with Yuan Shikai as president. "Thinking the revolution was over," Mao later told a biographer, "I resigned from the army and returned to my books."[2]

Mao Zedong was now nineteen years old and adrift in Changsha, unwilling to return to the confined life of Shaoshan village. Letters from home, however, made it clear that his family felt that he should get a job, or at least begin preparing himself for a professional career. Mao agreed, but he could not decide on any particular course of study. In quick succession he enrolled in a police academy, a school that taught soapmaking, and a law school, only to drop out of each after a few days.

On the advice of an acquaintance, he decided to become an economist—the new China, reasoned the two young men, would need educated experts to reshape its economy. But after enrolling in a school of economics, Mao discovered that all the classes were taught in English, a language of which he was ignorant. Once again he dropped out. Next he applied for admission to the First Hunan Middle School in Changsha, but he found it too old-fashioned and traditional for his taste. The school's strict discipline irked his free-thinking spirit, and the study of the classics seemed irrelevant to the new, modern China. Mao left the school in disgust after six months. He had decided to teach himself what he wanted to know.

Mao rented a bed in a cheap boardinghouse and began studying alone in the public library of Changsha. He arrived each morning as soon as the doors opened and stayed all day, leaving only to buy lunch from a street vendor. Like "an ox let loose in a vegetable garden," as he later told a friend, he devoured pile after pile of books.[3] Many were volumes of Chinese history and scholarship, but others were the works of Western writers translated into Chinese. He read books by biologist Charles Darwin, economist Adam Smith, and philosophers Jean-Jacques Rousseau and John Stuart Mill. World history and geography fascinated him. He studied a map of the world that hung on one of the library walls; it was the first map he had ever seen that showed China as just one nation among many.

Less than a year later, Mao was out of money. His father, impatient with Mao's aimless drifting, refused to give him an allowance. For some time Mao had been searching for a purpose and a profession. Now he decided to become a teacher. If he enrolled in a teachers training college, he would receive free food and lodging while he studied. His application to a teachers college in Changsha was accepted in 1913. Mao donned the blue wool gown of a student. Tall and thin, with large hands and feet, thoughtful eyes, and the habit of speaking slowly and deliberately, he took his place among two hundred other teachers in training. Mao spent five fruitful years in college. He not only continued his studies but also gained experience as a political activist.

Mao studied ethics—the branch of philosophy concerned with good and evil and with how people ought to behave—under a teacher named Yang Changji. Yang, who had studied in Europe, had a powerful influence on Mao. The student came to share the teacher's belief that modern, Western ideas and technologies could revitalize an ailing China. Mao also remained a devoted reader of newspapers, which he called "living history." Other students turned to him for summaries of world events: the progress of World War I, which raged in Europe from 1914 to 1918; the growth of the communist movement in Russia, leading to the 1917 revolution that toppled Russia's monarchy and brought the communists into power; and Japan's increasing aggression toward China as it sought to build a colonial empire in Asia.

In 1915 the Japanese government tried to make a deal with Yuan Shikai that would have given Japan control over China's economy. When word of Yuan's dealings with the Japanese reached the public, the Chinese people were outraged. All over the country army garrisons rose up in revolt against Yuan. Yuan died in June 1916, but by that time the Republic of China had collapsed. The country was left without an effective government. Army generals set themselves up as warlords, fighting over the provinces like dogs over bones. Sun Yatsen's followers, the Kuomintang (KMT), or Nationalist party, joined the fray.

During those tumultuous years, Mao Zedong was mastering the skills of leadership. His fellow students elected him head of the student union. Mao was an active leader. He boosted the union's tiny budget by selling snacks in the street, he organized protests against the college's corrupt principal, and he formed a student brigade to defend the school from bands of soldiers intent on looting. He also founded a night school for the factory workers of Changsha. His advertisement for the school read: "We are not wood or stone but men. We must seek a little knowledge if we are to be effective members of society."[4] Few workers answered his call, however, and the night school closed after several months.

Mao had better luck with the New People's Study Society (NPSS), a political group he helped to found. The NPSS brought together young men and women to discuss such subjects as democracy, science, and modernization. Inspired by the magazine *New Youth,* the members of the NPSS agreed that the customs and traditions of "old China" should be discarded in favor of political reforms and social changes. The reformers were not yet sure what shape those changes should take, but they were attracted to socialism, a political and economic theory that says that a country's resources, such as farmland, mines, and factories, should be owned by all the people or by the state rather than by private individuals or companies.

Socialism, with its overtones of collective living and economic equality, appealed to many young people in China in the 1910s, especially after the communist revolution in Russia succeeded in establishing a socialist state there. Mao Zedong believed that China was on the verge of a similar revolution, waiting only for a leader to emerge. "How can China come to have a great philosophical and ethical revolutionary like Russia's Tolstoy?" Mao once cried out at an NPSS meeting, referring to Russian writer Leo Tolstoy. "Who will purge the people's old thoughts and develop new thoughts?"[5]

Mao and two of his friends in the NPSS nicknamed themselves the "Three Heroes," after characters in one of Mao's favorite novels. Together they followed a course of physical training that Mao developed to train his will and his endurance. They slept outdoors in all kinds of weather, ran up and down mountains, and lived on a strict and frugal diet. These spartan habits, Mao believed, would make him strong in body and mind, and strength was needed to build a better China.

Mao graduated from school in 1918. The next year his mother died. At her funeral in Shaoshan village, he recited a poem he had written in her honor:

The power of her love came from true sincerity.
She never lied or was deceitful.
When we were sick she held our hands, her heart
*   full of sorrow,*
And she admonished us, "You should strive to be
*   good."*[6]

Mao's mother's death loosened the last of his ties to Shaoshan. His heart now lay with his mentor, Yang Changji, and with his dreams of a new China. Mao turned his attention northward to Beijing. Professor Yang had won a teaching post at Beijing University. From Beijing he wrote to the NPSS about a program that sent Chinese students to France to study. In the autumn of 1918, Mao and other NPSS members went to Beijing to apply for this program.

Some of Mao's friends did go to France. Mao could have gone with them, but he chose to remain in China. He felt that his time would be better spent learning more about his own country. But he soon discovered that China's capital was both cold and expensive. The best accommodations he could find was a room shared with seven other young men. They all slept on a large *kang*, a type of heated bed used in China's chilly northern provinces, and they were so crowded that Mao had to warn the bedmates on either side of him whenever he wanted to turn over. They also shared a single overcoat—the first Mao had ever worn—and took turns wearing it. Despite these discomforts, Mao was impressed by the beauty of the capital. Years later he recalled his awe at his first sight of Beijing's parks, with their ice-coated willows and millions of white plum blossoms.

There was another reason, too, for Mao to enjoy Beijing. He had fallen in love with Yang Kaihui, the delicate, scholarly daughter of Professor Yang. He did not yet consider marriage, however. Not only was he penniless, but he believed he had a role to play in China's future—even if he did not know exactly what that role would be—and he was not sure that marriage could fit into his plans.

Through Professor Yang, Mao got a job in the library of Beijing University. Many famous scholars used the library, and Mao yearned to talk with them, but as he later said, "They had no time to listen to an assistant librarian speaking southern dialect."[7] Although Mao did not formally enroll in the university, he was allowed to attend lectures. A series of lectures on Marxism fed his interest in socialism. (German philosopher Karl Marx, 1818–1883, had developed the political and economic theory that history was moving inevitably toward socialist revolution, and eventually toward classless, collective communism.) As Mao said later, "My interest in politics continued to increase, and my mind turned more and more radical. But just now I was still confused, looking for a road."[8]

Early in 1919, Mao traveled 800 miles (1,288 kilometers) to the port city of Shanghai on the eastern coast to bid farewell to a group of students who were sailing to France. Along the way he stopped to visit many famous historical sites, such as the birthplace of Confucius and the settings of his favorite novels. The trip was Mao's personal pilgrimage through his country's feudal past. He was not impressed with Shanghai, a bustling modern city of two million people. Shanghai was the foreigners' headquarters. A sign at the entry to the foreign residential quarter warned: "Dogs and Chinese Not Allowed."

Mao went home to Hunan province and became a part-time schoolteacher in Changsha. He devoted most of his time, however, to political activism. He helped organize dozens of student protests. Sometimes his groups demanded equal rights for women; sometimes they boycotted products made in Japan. Mao also edited and wrote for a weekly paper called the *Xiang River Review*. The paper urged that the last of the old, corrupt China be swept away in favor of a new society in which everyone would be equal. "The movement for the liberation of mankind has shot forward," wrote Mao in the first issue of the *Review*. "What are the things which we should not be afraid of? We should not be afraid of Heaven, of gods, of ghosts, of the dead, and of war lords and capitalists."[9]

Mao had left Beijing just before students there protested against certain provisions in the Treaty of Versailles, which ended World War I. The treaty gave

Students in Shanghai, the center of foreign power in China, march in support of the 1919 May Fourth movement. Their banners say, "Down with the traitors who buy Japanese goods."

Japan control of territory and trading privileges within China that had formerly belonged to Germany. Students and other nationalists were furious, insisting that Germany's Chinese holdings should have been returned to China. The Beijing demonstration of May 4, 1919, gave rise to the May Fourth Movement, a widespread surge of nationalism. The Movement's call for sweeping political and cultural change rekindled the revolutionary enthusiasm of many young Chinese men and women, including Mao Zedong.

For some time Mao had been eager for change—but unsure what form the "new China" should take. By 1920 his search was over. Like many others who were influenced by the May Fourth Movement, Mao became convinced that China must embrace socialism and become a communist state. He opened a bookstore that sold radical and socialist literature.

The May Fourth Movement stimulated interest in socialism among Chinese students, labor leaders, and intellectuals. In 1920 the Russian Communist party began sending representatives to China to guide the development of socialism and communism there. Socialist organizations sprang up in China's cities. Mao founded a Marxist society in Changsha; its members came from the New People's Study Society and from other student and worker groups that he had helped organize. Mao shared with them his fervent belief that China would soon experience a revolution like the one that had transformed Russia. "Heads will fall, heads will be chopped off, of course, of course," he told one acquaintance. "But just think how good communism is!"[10]

Busy though he was with political activities, Mao found time for his personal life. For some time he had been involved in a relationship with Yang Kaihui. After she moved from Beijing back to Changsha in 1920, the two were married. Their first child, a boy named Anying, was born in 1921. A second son, Anqing, would follow in 1923.

In July 1921 the Russian communist advisers invited a dozen Chinese Marxists to a secret meeting in Shanghai. Their purpose was momentous: to found the Chinese Communist party (CCP). Mao attended this historic meeting and from that time was recognized as one of the founders of communism in China. As party secretary for Hunan province, he enrolled many new members. Soon his two younger brothers and his younger sister, as well as many of his acquaintances, were working under his direction in communist organizations.

From the start, the Chinese communists faced a dilemma. Their Russian advisers, following Marx's doctrine, insisted that the socialist revolution would begin with the urban, industrial working class. But this approach to revolution had been formed in Europe, where there was a large industrial working class in the cities. Marxist theory did not fit the realities of China, which was primarily an agricultural nation. China did have mines, railroads, dockyards, and factories, but the total number of industrial workers was tiny compared with the masses of peasants who worked the land. Mao argued that the revolution should begin as the Taiping Rebellion had begun, among the rural peasants, the true backbone of China. For the time being, however, he was overruled. The leaders of the CCP continued to insist that the revolution would begin in the cities.

Another crucial issue for the CCP involved its relationship with Sun Yatsen and the Kuomintang. The Kuomintang, armed and organized for fighting, was far larger than the newly formed CCP. The two groups shared some goals. Both wanted to restore order to China, to end the rule of the warlords, and to curb Japanese aggression. But unlike the CCP, the Kuomintang was not committed to a socialist revolution—indeed, many of the Nationalist leaders were landowners or aristocrats who had no desire to see socialism take root in China. As a result, the communists distrusted the Nationalist party. They realized, however, that they had little chance of accomplishing anything unless they worked together with the powerful Kuomintang. So in 1924 the CCP allied itself with the Kuomintang. Mao Zedong was elected by his fellow communists to represent the CCP on the Kuomintang's leadership committee.

Mao spent the next few years in the large coastal cities of Shanghai and Guangzhou, writing articles for radical newspapers, organizing labor unions and protests, doing the work of the CCP and the Nationalist party. His wife and children remained in

Changsha; he saw little of them. Mao remained close to his brothers, however, and made several visits to Shaoshan village, especially after his father's death. Everywhere in the Hunan countryside, Mao saw signs that order and government had broken down. Centuries-old dams and irrigation canals were crumbling; judges and other officials had fled to the cities; flood and famine ravaged the peasantry.

But there were hopeful signs as well. The peasants, it seemed, had started the revolution on their own. In many places they had organized into crude fighting bands, seized the land from its rich owners, and divided it up among themselves. Mao's belief that the rural peasants were the source of revolutionary power was confirmed.

Meanwhile, the Nationalist army was building up its strength under the command of an able general named Chiang Kaishek, who emerged as the leader of the Kuomintang after Sun Yatsen died in early 1925. A few months afer Sun's death, British police in Shanghai killed some Chinese communists who were striking against a Japanese mill owner. When word spread that foreigners were killing Chinese, riots broke out. Resentment flared up against the hated foreigners. In Shanghai, Guangzhou, and elsewhere, strikes were declared. The Chinese people threw their support behind Chiang and the Nationalists, who promised to drive out both the foreigners and their puppets, the warlords. Chiang's army easily overthrew one of the chief warlords of the south.

Then, in 1926, Chiang launched a military expedition against the warlords of the north.

Mao Zedong now found himself, as historian Ross Terrill says, "out on a political limb."[11] He was a member of the CCP, and at the same time he held several important posts within the Nationalist party. Yet the fragile alliance between the communists and the Nationalists was breaking down. Nationalist leaders, including Chiang, made no secret of the fact that they did not intend to let communism take hold in China; Chiang even had some communists arrested. But Mao stayed involved with the Nationalist party because he thought that its leaders, unlike the top officials of the CCP, shared his belief in the importance of the rural peasants. Wrote Mao in 1926: "If the peasants do not arise and fight in the villages to overthrow the. . . landlord class, the power of the warlords and of imperialism can never be hurled down."[12]

Chiang's army swept north, kindling revolt as it marched. In the army's wake the peasants rose up against their oppressors. Landlords were killed, jailed, or driven away. The peasants burned the tax and rent lists, seized the land, and looted the houses of the rich. Mao rejoiced to see the peasants turning society upside down. "Every bit of the dignity and prestige built up by the landlords is being swept into the dust," he exulted.[13] The Kuomintang leaders, however, were considerably less pleased. They had no intention of conquering the warlords only to hand China over to the communists.

In the spring of 1927 the Nationalists decided not only to cut their ties to the CCP but to wipe out their former allies. Nationalist troops attacked the communist militia in Shanghai, killing as many as 5,000 CCP members. Similar attacks took place in Guangzhou, Beijing, and Hunan province. Communists fled into hiding or into exile. Within a few months, death and desertion had reduced the membership of the CCP from 70,000 to 5,000.

The communists fought back against the Nationalists, not just for their own survival but, as they saw it, for the soul of China. A communist force called the Red Army, hastily organized by a brilliant general named Zhu De, seized the city of Nanchang from the Kuomintang on August 1 but could not hold it. The desperate CCP leaders in Hunan put Mao Zedong in command of four Red Army regiments and ordered him to take Changsha from the tough, well-armed Kuomintang forces that controlled the city.

On the eve of battle, gazing across the river at the city where he had studied and worked as a hopeful student, Mao wrote a poem:

> *Eagles cleave the air,*
> *Fish glide in the limpid deep;*
> *Under freezing skies a million creatures contend*
> *   in freedom.*
> *Brooding over this immensity,*
> *I ask, on this boundless land,*
> *Who rules over man's destiny?* [14]

CHAPTER 4

THE LONG MARCH

The attack on Changsha never really got off the ground. Realizing that he could not capture the well-defended city, Mao disobeyed the orders of the CCP Central Committee and retreated from Changsha, harried at each step by Nationalist forces. He led his 1,000 dispirited followers south to a craggy, fog-shrouded peak called Well Mountain, in the Chingkang Mountains on the border of Hunan and Jiangxi provinces. There, like the outlaw heroes of his favorite books, Mao holed up, and soon the remnants of the Red Army were joined by several outlaw bands. In faded and dirty clothes, with a tangle of long hair and a beard that covered the prominent mole on his chin, Mao looked like a bandit chieftain himself. But the society that he created atop Well Mountain was orderly and followed strict principles.

Mao's band of stragglers grew as people came from all over the surrounding region to join him. He welcomed everyone, including criminals and army deserters. "Everyone had his strong points," he once said. "Even the lame, the deaf, and the blind could all help in the revolutionary struggle."[1] Mao's rules for his followers were simple: No one was allowed to steal from the peasants—the army would pay for the food and other goods it took from the people of the countryside. Looting was not permitted—everything taken from the rich landlords was turned over to Mao's staff.

Above all, Mao was determined that everyone be educated in socialist principles, so that the soldiers would know that they were fighting not just to wrest power from the Nationalists but to establish a new order in China. Landlords and rich peasants, too, were forced to attend lectures in socialist doctrine; those who resisted or objected were shot. Mao was equally severe on his own followers when they let him down. A few years later he had 3,000 Red Army men shot for saying that Mao should step aside in favor of another CCP leader.

Maoism—Mao Zedong's brand of socialism and revolution—began to take shape on Well Mountain. One key ingredient of Maoism was Mao's insistence that China must follow a course shaped by its own history and conditions, not a blueprint handed down by Russian Marxists. Marxism had grown out of the theorizing of a middle-class German intellectual, but Maoism would be firmly rooted in the experience of the Chinese peasants. Mao believed that the revolutionary army should be drawn from the peasant population, which then would support the army and its goals. He drew upon a traditional Chinese image to make this point, saying, "The army moves through the people as the fish move through the water."

Another important element of Maoism was Mao's emphasis on educating the people—forcibly, if necessary—in the principles of socialism and revolution. He did not want the grudging support of the masses; he wanted their enthusiastic understanding, and he believed that once his ideas and goals were explained, everyone would embrace them.

From the time he arrived in the Chingkang Mountains, Mao was at odds with the Central Committee of the CCP, from which he was supposed to take orders. The Central Committee and its Russian advisers still believed that the socialist revolution should be carried out in the cities, not in the countryside, and Mao was criticized for forming a rural stronghold. In addition, Mao made some members of the Central Committee nervous. They did not like to see such an independent-minded leader setting up his own power base, complete with loyal armed followers, so far from their control. Mao was often scornful of the Central Committee's directives. Sometimes he simply ignored them, pretending that he had never received them.

In early 1928, Mao received orders that he could not ignore: He was told to attack the Nationalists in Hunan province. But as soon as his Red Army troops left Well Mountain, they were cut to pieces by the well-armed Nationalists, who then swooped in behind Mao's back and captured his base. Mao was forced to retreat under fire and fight long and hard to reclaim Well Mountain.

Mao's forces were aided by those of the communist general Zhu De. Once they had retaken Well Mountain, Mao and Zhu merged their armies into a unified force. Their union was a crucial moment in the Chinese revolution. Mao was an inspired thinker and long-range planner, while Zhu was a brilliant military commander. Together they provided strong leadership. Lin Baio, one of Zhu's officers, was another outstanding commander who threw his support behind Mao. Soon Lin became a leading general in his own right.

Still, Mao was at odds with the Central Committee, who disapproved of the shifty, nimble guerrilla tactics that Mao used to drive the Nationalists out of Well Mountain. The Central Committee ordered another full frontal assault on the Nationalists in May 1928. Although Mao argued against it, Zhu led the Red Army back into Hunan. Once again the communists took a beating; once again Well Mountain fell to the Nationalists; and once again Mao, Zhu, and Lin had to struggle desperately to retake the base.

Yet Mao found time for love as well as war in 1928. At a CCP meeting he met an eighteen-year-old girl named He Zizhen, an ardent communist who represented the youthful, forward-looking energy of the "new China." Soon she and Mao became lovers.

In 1929, Mao moved his followers down from the Chingkang Mountains to establish a larger and better-supplied base in Jiangxi province. He called this base a "soviet" (a self-governing state inside China, modeled on the Russian soviets, which were governed by councils of workers and soldiers). Within a few years the Jiangxi soviet had expanded to include seventeen counties.

Jiangxi was not the only communist stronghold in China, and Mao was not the only communist leader who put theory into practice by bringing territory under communist rule. A number of other soviets were set up in various parts of China, but the Jiangxi soviet was the largest.

Within the soviets, life was reorganized along socialist lines. Property was seized from the landlords and turned into collective farms worked by teams of peasants. Taxes were lifted, and the peasants formed "cooperatives" to govern themselves under the supervision of the CCP. The peasants' living and working conditions improved dramatically, while landlords and others who were deemed by the CCP to be enemies of the peasant class were subjected to terrorism, arrest, mass trials, and execution.

Despite his success in Jiangxi, Mao was locked in a power struggle with rivals in the CCP. When the Central Committee moved from Shanghai to the Jiangxi soviet, Mao's powers were sharply limited. The Central Committee took the top army command away from Mao and gave it to Zhou Enlai. Mao was reduced to a minor role in party affairs. For a time he was even placed under house arrest by the pro-Russian faction that dominated the CCP Central Committee. During this time Mao had several serious bouts of malaria, a potentially fatal disease transmitted by mosquito bites. Some of the self-confident young party leaders regarded the middle-aged, sickly Mao as a washed-up failure. Mao waited, watched, and bided his time.

Meanwhile, the civil war between the communists and the Nationalists raged on. Chiang Kaishek remained firm in his determination to wipe out Chinese communism. In 1930, Mao's sister was killed by the Nationalists in Changsha. Yang Kaihui, his wife, was also killed; when Mao learned of her death, he married He Zizhen.

Chiang's forces made several attempts to crush the Jiangxi base, but the Red Army turned them back. Then, in 1931, Chiang had to abandon his assault on Jiangxi to confront another foe: Japanese forces that invaded and occupied Manchuria. By 1933, however, Chiang had arranged a truce with the Japanese and was free to turn his attention back to the communists. He came south to Jiangxi with a million soldiers and by October 1933 had launched a massive campaign against the soviet. The Red Army was steadily driven back, until by the summer of 1934 the communists controlled only six counties.

Poor strategy on the part of Zhou and other CCP leaders played into Chiang's hands. Although

*C*hiang Kaishek, Sun Yatsen's successor as leader of the Nationalist party, was fiercely opposed to communism. He sought to trap Mao and the Chinese communists within "walls of fire."

Mao had argued that the communist forces should remain mobile and agile, they had done just the opposite, entrenching themselves in their base and building forts all around it. Now Chiang ordered his troops to build more forts, barricades, and trenches around the base, isolating it from the outside world and trapping the communists inside. Chiang turned the communists' own defenses into a trap that he called "walls of fire."

Food and medicine ran short inside the base. Chiang's bombers and heavy artillery guns hammered away at the besieged communists. The CCP leaders decided to break through the "walls of fire" and abandon Jiangxi to regroup somewhere else. Dozens of rival plans were put forward. In the end they decided to leave a small garrison in Jiangxi and make a break for a soviet base in northern Hunan province.

About 100,000 people prepared for the exodus from Jiangxi. Most were soldiers, but some were packhorse grooms, porters to carry supplies (including printing presses, furniture, and the party archives), and the family members of senior party officials. He Zizhen, who was pregnant at the time, was one of the women who would make the journey. The majority of the marchers were young. Fewer than 5 percent of them were forty years old or more, and more than half were under twenty-four. Some were only twelve or thirteen. But because it had been decreed that only children old enough to walk could come along, the two young sons that He Zizhen had borne

Mao were left behind in the care of a peasant family. It is not known whether Mao ever tried to find them again; their fate is a mystery.

On October 19, 1934, the Red Army began its desperate attack on the Kuomintang's "walls of fire." Ten days later the vanguard broke through, and the long Red line streamed westward. Mao's brother Zetan was one of those who remained behind to defend the Jiangxi base; he was killed when the base fell a few months later.

The communists made their way west and north, fighting a series of battles with the Nationalists, who spied out their route from airplanes. A devastating encounter took place at the Xiang River in southern Hunan, where the communist forces were attacked by Chiang's superior army as they tried to cross the river. In a week of fighting, the Red Army lost between 30,000 and 50,000 men. The CCP leaders realized that they could not continue to fight their way northward; Chiang's army outnumbered theirs six to one. The Central Committee fell to arguing about what they should do.

At this point, with the leadership of the party in disarray and the army battered and discouraged, Mao came out of the shadows and began to take charge. He convinced the army to abandon its cumbersome baggage in favor of traveling light. Instead of a fixed line of march that was easy for Chiang to predict, Mao adopted guerrilla tactics, ordering sudden changes in direction, marches and countermarches,

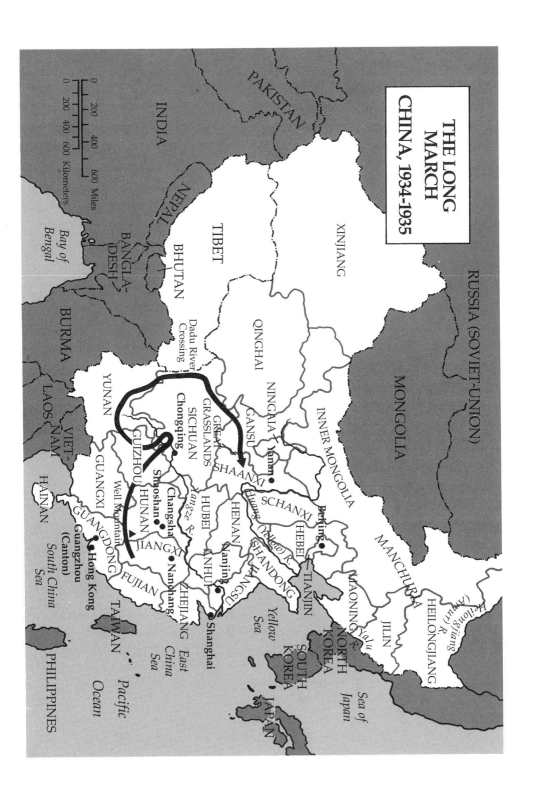

The grueling Long March brought Mao Zedong (center) to the fore as the unquestioned leader of China's communists. His principal lieutenants were Zhou Enlai (left) and Zhu De (right).

and frequent backtracking. He also split up the army into several columns to confuse the Nationalists.

The communists moved south into mountainous Guizhou province. Catching both the Nationalists and the warlords unprepared, the Red Army captured a city called Zunyi. There the CCP leaders called a conference to decide on their next move. But the Zunyi conference was more than a planning session. It was a battle for control of the Chinese Communist party and the Red Army.

Mao dominated the conference, pointing out that the inflexible methods of the Russian-dominated leaders had led the army into disaster. Zhou Enlai and Zhu De supported Mao, who emerged from the conference as the supreme leader of both the CCP and the army. Mao gave the communists a new goal: They would go to Shaanxi province in the north, joining forces along the way with Red Army troops from elsewhere in China. In Shaanxi they would organize to fight the Japanese, for Mao insisted that the most important task facing the Chinese people was to drive out the invaders and secure China's borders. He also believed that fighting the Japanese was good policy. Once the Chinese people saw that the communists were dedicated to the war against Japan, they would support the CCP in its struggle against the Nationalists.

But Mao's columns could not march straight north to Shaanxi—that route was blocked by Chiang and the Kuomintang. So Mao ordered his columns south through Guizhou into the steaming rain forests of Yunnan, on the Vietnamese border. When

Chiang sent the Nationalist forces charging south into Yunnan on Mao's heels, Mao swiftly reversed course and, bypassing the oncoming enemy, hurried into northwestern Yunnan, a remote, mountainous region on the border of Tibet.

To proceed north into Sichuan province on the next stage of their journey, the communists had to cross the Yangtze River, which pours from the Tibetan plateau through a steep gorge. There were no bridges; the river could be crossed only on ferryboats. Hoping to keep the communists bottled up south of the Yangtze where he could pick them off at his leisure, Chiang ordered all the boats in Mao's line of march to be burned.

Mao came up with a crafty solution worthy of one of his favorite novels: He sent one unit south along the riverbank to distract Chiang's scouts, ordered a second group to begin building a bridge as another distraction, and led a third group 85 miles (137 kilometers) downstream to a Kuomintang garrison. Wearing captured Nationalist uniforms, this third group managed to get inside the garrison and seize it, along with its ferry boats. Within a week the entire army had marched south and crossed the river.

The marchers were now in west Sichuan, a rugged, almost inaccessible region inhabited by Tibetans and other non-Chinese minorities. Mao dickered for safe passage with these warlike tribes, once going so far as to order one of his generals to drink a bowl of chicken blood to seal a bargain with a local chieftain. Ahead lay a formidable obstacle: the Dadu River, knifing through ice-capped mountain ranges, swollen with spring snowmelt. No boat could cross the Dadu, and there was only one bridge, a set of chains with planks laid across them 200 feet (60 meters) above the torrent. The far side of the bridge was guarded by Nationalist troops, who had removed the planks.

In one of the most remarkable feats in the history of warfare, twenty-two young Red Army soldiers volunteered to storm the bridge. They swung across the river hand-to-hand from the chains, carrying grenades and rifles, under fire from the Nationalists. Only five of them made it, but they attacked the Nationalist post while others swung across in a second wave. The Nationalists fled in dismay—all but about a hundred of them, who were so impressed with the communists' heroism that they asked to join the Red Army.

Once across the Dadu, Mao led his column to a meeting with another Red Army that was marching west from Hubei province. The route led over the Great Snow Mountains, a series of steep 17,000-foot (5,200-meter) ranges, where hundreds of marchers dropped dead in their tracks from cold, exhaustion, and hunger. Their bodies were left behind, covered by drifting snow.

Mao Zedong did his best to keep up his troops' spirits. He rode or walked among them, chatting and telling jokes, and he made a tea of hot peppers and ginger that helped them withstand the bitter cold. Mao spent little time with He Zizhen during the march. His few free moments were spent reading his beloved *Story of the Marshes* or writing poems, such as one inspired by the grand landscape across which he and his followers crawled like ants:

Mountains!
Like great waves surging in a crashing sea,
Like a thousand stallions
In full gallop in the heat of battle.

Mountains!
Piercing the blue of heaven, your barbs
unblunted!
The skies would fall
But for your strength supporting. [2]

In June, Mao's army of 45,000 joined Zhang Guotao's army of 50,000 in northwestern Sichuan. Mao wanted the united force to press on northward to Shaanxi, but Zhang argued that they should build a base on the western border of China. Unable to agree and mistrustful of one another, the two leaders separated. Zhang went west, farther into the highlands on the Tibetan border. Mao went northeast toward Shaanxi but suffered a grave blow: Zhu De and his troops went with Zhang. Mao and his commanders Lin Baio and Zhou Enlai were left with about 30,000 men. They now had to cross the Great Grasslands on Sichuan's northern border—a more desperate ordeal, survivors later declared, than any of the mountains, rivers, or battles that had gone before.

The Great Grasslands are a foggy, boggy swamp several hundred miles across. Cold, wet, reduced to eating grass and fungus, covered with infected sores from the dirty water, sinking without a trace into the muck if they strayed off the narrow footpath, the Red Army slogged onward. The Grasslands were inhabited by a people called the Man, who bitterly opposed the army's passage through their domain and peppered the column with poisoned arrows. The communists were unable to buy provisions, for the queen of the Man announced that she would boil alive any of her subjects who aided the Reds, so the desperate marchers stole and killed to get food. Thousands died in the crossing.

In October 1935, one year after leaving Jiangxi, Mao Zedong and his followers stumbled into Shaanxi province. They were met by riders with the red star of communism on their caps—members of the Shaanxi soviet. After an extraordinary journey of 6,000 miles (9,656 kilometers), Mao had reached his new stronghold with 20,000 survivors, one-fifth of those who had left Jiangxi.

The Long March, as the trek from Jiangxi to Shaanxi came to be called, was one of the most extraordinary expeditions in military annals. Yet it was not a single, unified body of people under Mao's leadership from start to finish, as it has sometimes been portrayed. The Long March started as a desperate retreat from Jiangxi, and for a while it had no real destination. Even the route of the Long March is hard to trace clearly because so many army divisions under various commanders joined and left the march, or traveled by alternative routes.

But the path followed by Mao Zedong *was* the Long March in the eyes of the Chinese people, because the march made Mao a legend. The march also exposed millions of people to the Red Army and to Mao's revolutionary goals. At every stop along the way the Reds held rallies, telling the people about the need to fight the Japanese and to bring a new social order to China. Sometimes they gave practical demonstrations of land reform, confiscating the land and property of the wealthy and giving it to the poor. Understandably, these demonstrations were popular with the peasants. In many places the Reds set up militia bases or left party members behind to spread the revolution.

In the years that followed, the Long March was recognized as a pivotal event in the history of modern China. Maoists regarded it as a sacred pilgrimage. Those who survived it were national heroes. To Mao, the Long March was like an episode from the ancient days or from a heroic epic. He said, "Since heaven was divided from earth and the Three Sovereigns and the Five Emperors reigned, has there ever been in history a long march like ours?"[3]

Mao Zedong in Shaanxi province, 1937. Already the Long March had made Mao into a larger-than-life hero. Soon this "son of peasants" would be locked in a bitter battle with Chiang Kaishek for control of China.

CHAPTER 5 THE TRIUMPH

The communists spent about a year consolidating their base in Shaanxi. By 1937, Mao had set up the headquarters of the CCP in the town of Yanan. Over the centuries hundreds of homes and temples have been carved into the yellow hills of Yanan, and Mao lived in several of these caves during the decade he spent in Shaanxi. Mao did not lead the Red Army into battle; he directed military and party affairs from his cave.

Mao put his ideas into practice in Yanan. The Red soldiers brought increasingly more of Shaanxi under communist control. They cut taxes, took land from the rich and gave it to the poor, and worked side by side in the fields with the peasants. The CCP introduced literacy and medical care to people who had never seen a teacher or a doctor. Everyone dressed alike in peasant clothing—the loose-fitting blue trousers and jacket that became the uniform of the new

China. Soldiers and peasants shared a mood of hope, energy, and equality that was called "the Yanan spirit." One historian has said of the days in Yanan, "People felt, for a time, that they were building a new world with their own hands."[1]

Word spread of what was happening in Yanan, and from all over China people came to see it for themselves. Many joined the movement. They included students, artists, intellectuals and reformers, peasants, and even outlaws. Some foreigners came to Yanan, too, curious about the revolution that was reshaping this corner of northwest China. British, American, and European journalists visited Mao in his cave and gave the rest of the world its first detailed accounts of Chinese communism, Mao Zedong, and the Long March.

Some of these foreign visitors were disturbed by the conformity imposed by the CCP; they called the identically clad workers "blue ants." These observers also criticized the violence against landlords and other "class enemies." Other visitors, however, praised Mao and the movement for throwing off the age-old shackles of peasant repression. "Mass rallies and propaganda talks might be boring," wrote historian Eric Chou in *Mao Tse-tung: The Man and the Myth,* "but they were at least tolerable when compared with the peasants' previous experiences of living under the local warlords."[2]

Mao received visitors in his cave, which was furnished with a few simple pieces of furniture. He relaxed by tending his tomato garden. A lifelong heavy smoker, he also tried producing his own tobacco, although each supply convoy brought him a special shipment of quality cigarettes—his one luxury.

Mao's wife, He Zizhen, soon passed out of his life. She had suffered greatly during the Long March and had a mental breakdown in Shaanxi. Mao shipped her off to Moscow, along with their daughter, born during the Long March, and his two sons from his earlier marriage to Yang Kaihui. He Zizhen was placed in a mental asylum in Moscow; later she was transferred to an asylum in Shanghai. Mao never saw her again after 1937. He had found a new love, an actress from Shanghai named Jiang Qing.

Mao's relationship with Jiang caused a storm of protest in the Central Committee. Mao's colleagues claimed that it looked bad for the party leader to cast aside a wife who was a dedicated communist and a veteran of the Long March in favor of an actress whose involvement with the party was quite recent. But Mao had his way, and by 1939 he was living with Jiang. No official record exists of Mao's divorce from He Zizhen or his marriage to Jiang Qing, although Jiang was always treated as his wife. Their first child, a daughter, was born in 1941.

Mao chats with two boy soldiers of the Red Army in Yanan, 1939. The "Yanan spirit" of the late 1930s drew world attention to Mao and his followers.

While Mao enjoyed considerable freedom in his private life, he denied it to the population under his control. The party began to frown on sexual relations between unmarried people, and new marriage laws made it difficult for people to obtain divorces. At the same time, other laws gave new freedoms to women. Arranged marriages were prohibited, and women were given the right to own property.

All the while, Mao remained focused on Japan, which was becoming increasingly aggressive toward China. To the dismay of some communists, he was even willing to make an alliance with the hated Nationalists against the Japanese. Mao explained that the survival of China was more important than the conflict between the communists and the Nationalists: "We cannot even discuss communism," he said, "if we are robbed of a country in which to practice it."[3]

In 1937, Mao and Chiang Kaishek signed an agreement to suspend their war against one another and join forces against the Japanese. The ink was barely dry on the agreement when Japanese troops moved south from Manchuria, striking at Shanghai and other Chinese cities in a full-scale invasion. The communists in the north and the Nationalists in the south and west fought valiantly, but Japan's war machine was powerful. The struggle dragged on and on, and Chiang lost ground. The communists, however, fought their usual dogged guerrilla war and were quite effective. To many Chinese, it seemed that the communists were fighting harder than the Nationalists for Chinese liberty. Popular support for the communists began to grow.

During this time, Mao Zedong began to appear a larger-than-life, godlike figure. Posters displaying his handwriting and his portrait bloomed in public places, and popular songs praising him spread through the army. Whether this cultlike worship of Mao arose from his peasant admirers, as he claimed, or was deliberately engineered by Mao and his cronies, as some historians have suggested, the result was the same: Revolution, communism, progress, right thinking—all came to have Mao's face, and that face was everywhere.

The alliance between the communists and the Nationalists cracked in 1940 when Chiang broke the agreement and attacked one of the communist armies. Many Chinese, even those who had no love for the communists, were outraged that Chiang Kaishek, who claimed to be a patriot, had turned his guns against patriotic Chinese soldiers instead of fighting the Japanese. A showdown between Mao and Chiang appeared imminent.

By this time, World War II had broken out in Europe. In the Pacific, Japan's ambition to conquer all of eastern Asia led to the "Three Alls" campaign in China in 1941—the motto of the Japanese troops was "Kill all, loot all, burn all." When Japan attacked the U.S. naval base at Pearl Harbor in Hawaii, the United States entered the war and began supplying China with military and financial aid against Japan. The aid went to the Nationalists, because Chiang insisted that the Americans deal only with him and not with the communists. At first the U.S. government tried to persuade Chiang to cooperate with the communists, but Chiang was adamant: The United States could not support both parties. Its support went to the Nationalists, and Mao Zedong's friendliness toward America began to cool.

In 1945 the CCP held a meeting for representatives of China's 1.2 million communists (the largest communist party in the world outside the Soviet Union). Mao was elected chairman of the CCP, its most powerful position. His key lieutenants were Zhou Enlai and Liu Shaoqi, a Long March veteran whom Mao had known since his days as a student organizer in Hunan. Liu, a skilled planner, wrote the party's constitution, and the suave, articulate Zhou handled the party's relations with foreign journalists, intellectuals, and diplomats.

World War II ended in 1945 with Japan's surrender to the United States. Japanese troops withdrew from China, leaving the stage set for a new civil war between the communists and the Nationalists. In August 1945, Chiang invited Mao to visit him in Chongqing, Sichuan, to discuss China's future. The flight to Chongqing was Mao's first trip in an airplane. Looking down, he wrote:

The mountains dance like silver snakes
And the highlands charge like waxen-hued
* elephants,*

Vying with heaven in stature.
On a fine day, the land,
Clad in white, adorned in red,
Grows more enchanting.[4]

The "white" of the poem is snow, but it also represents the Nationalists, who were called the Whites. The "red" that adorns the land may refer to reddish-brown soil or to the light of sunset reflected on snow, but it is also a reference to communism. The Reds, Mao was saying, had become part of the Chinese landscape. The communists now controlled territory inhabited by nearly a hundred million people, and the Red Army was a million strong.

Mao proved himself a showman in Chongqing. He posed for pictures with Chiang, drank to Chiang's health, and loudly proclaimed his eagerness to work with Chiang to build a peaceful, united China. Many observers and foreign journalists went away convinced that Mao respected Chiang and would cooperate with him in a joint government. Yet in private Mao said, "Chiang Kaishek has lost his soul, he is merely a corpse and no one believes in him any more." [5]

The agreement that Mao and Chiang signed after forty-three days of negotiations was hollow. In reality, Chiang would not cooperate with Mao as long as Mao controlled the Red Army, and Mao would not give up the army, for he knew that he would have no authority without it. As he was fond of saying, "From the barrel of a gun grows political power."[6]

I n Chongqing, Mao (left) shares a toast with
his longtime foe, Chiang (right). The
agreement signed by the two men was meaningless;
their forces were again at war within months.

The fighting began in 1946, when Chiang's Nationalist forces tried to drive Lin Baio's communist army out of Manchuria. Still reeling from the Japanese occupation, China was again torn by civil war. Lin Baio commanded the communists' northern armies, and Mao left his Shaanxi base to command the southern forces of the Red Army, which at this time was renamed the People's Liberation Army (PLA). Chiang's forces outnumbered the PLA, but by late 1948 the Nationalists were on the run.

The United States and the Soviet Union were deeply interested in China's civil war. The Americans backed Chiang. The Soviets naturally supported the communists, but Joseph Stalin, the leader of the Soviet Union, was afraid that a communist victory in China might push the United States into war against world communism. Stalin cautioned Mao not to anger the United States. Although Mao felt great admiration and respect for Stalin, he disregarded the Soviet leader's advice. For Mao, China's interests always came first, and he was more concerned with establishing a communist state in China than with the fate of world communism.

Mao launched an all-out offensive against the Nationalists, taking city after city. Lin Baio's army besieged the ancient city of Beijing until the Kuomintang general surrendered. PLA troops marched into Beijing in triumph. Many of them were rural peasants who had never seen a large city before. They gawked at the sights, and those who were unfa-

miliar with electricity tried to light their cigarettes from lightbulbs.

By September 1949 the long struggle between the Chinese communists and the Kuomintang was over. All of China belonged to the CCP and the PLA. Chiang and the Nationalists fled to Taiwan, an island off the Chinese coast, where they set up a government in exile. The CCP Central Committee went to Beijing to begin ruling the country.

Pictures of Mao and banners cheering the "new China" appeared all over Beijing. Overnight, the Nationalist newspaper *North China Daily News* became the communist *People's Daily*. The city sizzled with curiosity and excitement when Mao arrived. Yet he did not immediately make public appearances. He set up his headquarters with Jiang Qing in a graceful royal pavilion in the Forbidden City, moving his books and his spittoon into a set of elegant, high-ceilinged rooms. Then, on October 1, he climbed onto the Gate of Heavenly Peace to proclaim the birth of a new nation, the People's Republic of China (PRC).

Mao Zedong had become the most powerful man in the most populous nation in the world. The CCP ruled China, and he ruled the CCP. For de-

With Mao's portrait and the red star of communism as their banners, the victorious soldiers of the People's Liberation Army march through the streets of Beijing in June 1949.

cades Mao and the communists had lived by their wits and their guns in villages and on the fringes of the country. Now they were in the seat of power. They faced the challenge of running the whole nation. Mao had foreseen that victory would bring new challenges. Earlier he had told his followers, "We shall soon put aside some of the things we know well, and be compelled to do things we don't know well."[7]

CHAPTER 6

CONSTANT STRUGGLE

One of Mao Zedong's first acts as the new leader of China was to go to Moscow to meet with Stalin. The journey was both Mao's first diplomatic visit to another country and his first trip outside China. On one level, the trip was a success for Mao: The Soviet Union agreed to give the equivalent of 300 million American dollars in financial aid to China. Yet the mission was also a disappointment. Mao had hoped for more aid, and he resented the fact that Stalin treated him as a pupil or a supplicant rather than as an equal. Furthermore, it took Mao two months to persuade Stalin to agree to provide the aid, and the price was steep. Mao had to let part of Mongolia, which he regarded as a province of China, become an independent nation under Soviet protection.

On his return to Beijing, Mao had little time to fret about the snub he had received in Moscow. The year after the founding of the People's Republic of China, the new nation went to war on two fronts.

On the Korean peninsula between China and Japan, fighting broke out between North Korea, which was supported by the Soviet Union, and South Korea, supported by the United States. American troops went to Korea to help the southern forces against the northern armies. Although Mao warned that China would not allow a foreign army to approach its borders, the American general Douglas MacArthur advanced to the Yalu River, the border between China and North Korea. In response, Mao ordered China to enter the war as North Korea's ally in October 1950.

Three years of fierce fighting followed. Thousands were killed on both sides, including Mao's son Anying (his other son with Yang Kaihui, Anqing, was mentally ill). In the end, the war changed nothing in Korea: The border between North Korea and South Korea remained exactly where it had been before the fighting started. But the relationship between the People's Republic of China and the United States had worsened dramatically. Having fought against each other in Korea, each country now regarded the other as a dangerous, implacable foe. The U.S. government renewed its support of Chiang Kaishek's regime on Taiwan and refused to allow the PRC to have the seat allotted to China in the United Nations.

While China was entering the Korean War on its northeastern border, it also sent armies marching southwest to invade Tibet in 1950. The Dalai Lama, the spiritual and political leader of the Tibetan people, was permitted to remain in Tibet, but only under Chinese control. In 1959, when Chinese forces stepped up their campaign to wipe out Tibetan Buddhism and crush the pro-independence movement in Tibet, the Dalai Lama fled to India. Since that time China has remained firmly in control of Tibet. Mao Zedong and the CCP described the Chinese occupation of Tibet as China's rightful return to its ancient borders (for several periods in history Tibet was under Chinese dominion). The Tibetans and many people outside China, however, regard China's presence in Tibet as the brutal invasion of a peaceful, autonomous land.

Domestic affairs also received Mao's attention as soon as the PRC was established. He began a series of reforms aimed at reshaping Chinese society. There were campaigns against corruption, bribery, tax evasion, stealing government property, and other wasteful practices that had been all too common under the chaotic rule of the warlords. But to millions of China's poor peasants, the most important of Mao's changes was land reform. The policy that Mao had followed inside the soviets was now applied to the whole country. Land was taken from landlords and the rich and given to poor families.

Mao did not intend for every Chinese farmer to own land. His long-term vision was of a China with no private property, a place where peasants lived and worked communally on large state-owned farms. Redistribution of land to the poor was only a short-term measure between landlord ownership and communal farming. But the peasants did not know this, and they thought the land was theirs to keep. Grown men cried with joy to possess their own small plots.

At the same time, across the country, the peasants took the law into their own hands in what has been called "the settling of accounts movement."[1] The poor took savage revenge on the rich, arming themselves with whatever weapons came to hand and turning against landlords, merchants, and others whom they perceived as enemies. Millions were killed, often viciously. One peasant told an American writer about torturing the rich: "All you had to do to make a man talk was to heat an iron bar in the fire," he said, "but the women were tougher. They would rather die than tell us where their gold was hidden."[2]

Mao Zedong neither encouraged nor discouraged the violence. Eric Chou, one of Mao's biographers, says that although land reform in China brought more deaths than many wars, "the loss of human lives did not seem to bother Mao, for a few years later he casually admitted that the land reform had been carried out with 'some unavoidable errors like any other mass movement.' He put the number of deaths between six and seven million, as if it were nothing unusual."[3]

Thought reform was even more sweeping than land reform. Mao and the CCP refused to tolerate dissent or opposition to their programs. The CCP set up political study groups in every school, factory, village, and neighborhood to "educate" people in socialist doctrine. Those who disagreed with the party line were "re-educated"—browbeaten and threatened into making public "confessions." As historian Chou notes: "In other words, most people were converted into informants, informing against one another. It did not matter whether they merely picked up some gossip or had some wrong ideas, they had to pass them on to the party functionaries who were assigned to the study groups. The frightening aspect of the whole process was that the innocent could be incriminated without a shred of evidence."[4] Millions of people were imprisoned or sent to labor camps simply because the CCP accused them of "wrong thinking." Like other totalitarian regimes, the CCP believed that the state owned everything—even people's thoughts.

Mao began to display a streak of anti-intellectualism. He was scornful of those who merely wrote and taught, sometimes ordering poets and professors to work cleaning toilets or digging ditches. He banned China's classical literature and even ordered his old favorites, novels such as *The Romance of the Three Kingdoms*, to be rewritten from a socialist point of view. "It was clear to Mao," says Eric Chou, "that he could not afford to allow others to think independently or differently. He must be the one who provided all the answers for humankind."[5]

In 1957, Mao seemed to reverse himself. Announcing that vigorous debate about issues and ideas was a good thing, he introduced a campaign called

"Let a Hundred Flowers Bloom," which was supposed to encourage people to voice their honest opinions. Mao expected to hear a chorus of praise for all that he and the CCP had accomplished, and he was unpleasantly surprised by the sharp criticism he received from some intellectuals for his thought-reform policies. Abruptly reversing himself once again, Mao launched a new campaign to pluck the "poisonous weeds" of improper ideas from among the "fragrant flowers" of good CCP thought.

Such shifts in policy were typical of Mao. What he approved one day he might disapprove the next, and a party official who loudly and publicly agreed with Mao's position on Tuesday might find himself in disgrace when Mao changed his mind on Wednesday. Mao shifted course frequently to keep people guessing about his motives and plans. His unpredictability helped him to play factions against one another, thus preventing other top party officials and generals from gaining too much power at his expense. "He sought to divide and rule," says Eric Chou, "mainly to strengthen his personal power."[6]

When Mao and the CCP came to power, China's economy had been reduced to a shambles by decades of war, civil unrest, and weak and corrupt government. The communists embarked on a plan to rebuild the economy through modernization and industrialization. Their goal was to make China not only self-sufficient but a leader among nations. In the early years of communist rule, China's economy did improve, as the turmoil of war and revolution ebbed and people settled down to work on farms and in factories. In 1958, however, Mao decided that faster progress was needed. He announced a five-year economic plan that he called the "Great Leap Forward." The plan was supposed to propel China dramatically into the future.

All factories became the property of the state, although in some cases the former owners were allowed to remain as managers at a small salary. The state also asserted its claim to ownership of the entire countryside. Individually owned farms were to be abolished in favor of collectives, or commmunal farms. Furthermore, these rural collectives would also make steel in thousands of small furnaces, build their own machinery, and construct their own dams, bridges, and even hospitals as needed. Mao did not want to rely on the specialized knowledge of experts in industry and technology—he wanted to prove that the ordinary people of China could do everything that needed to be done.

At first the Great Leap Forward seemed like a huge success. Reports from around the country told of impressive grain harvests and steel production. But many of these reports were false or exaggerated. In fact, the Great Leap Forward was a failure. Instead of leaping ahead, China stumbled. Most of the steel produced in the small communal forges was of such poor quality that it was not good for anything, and a number of the dams and bridges built by untrained peasant brigades soon collapsed. The rural population resented being forced onto collective farms. Now that China's peasants had finally gotten land of their own, they wanted to hang onto it, not turn it over to the state.

The people also hated some of the party's other innovations. For example, Mao introduced a program of communal dining. He claimed that it was more efficient for large groups of people to cook and eat together than to do so as single families. In addition, the communal meals gave the party a chance to lecture the diners about socialism, either through local spokespersons or through the loudspeakers that sprang up all over China, constantly blaring forth party slogans and speeches. But the people who were assigned to communal dining halls complained that they wanted to eat their meals in the old way, with their families in their own homes. The people's participation in the new communal life was often less than enthusiastic.

In 1960, China entered the "Three Bitter Years," a time of economic setbacks. Harvests were so bad that parts of the country suffered famine; poor planning led to shortages of raw materials; and the output of manufactured goods such as clothing and shoes declined.

Mao shared nothing of his personal life with the public during these years. He and Jiang Qing continued to live in the pavilion Mao had chosen in

A propaganda photo from 1960 shows peasants on a collective farm in eastern China happily gathering for a meal in a communal eating hall. In reality, most Chinese objected to the communal meals—as well as to turning their hard-won land over to the state.

Beijing's royal compound, with other party officials living nearby. In addition to Li Na and Li Min, the daughters of Mao and Jiang, Mao's household included the son of Mao's brother Zemin, who had been killed by a warlord in western China in 1943.

Jiang Qing was ambitious, but she had not yet played a role in public life. At the time of his separation from He Zizhen, Mao had promised the CCP not to allow Jiang Qing to become a power in the party or the government. During the early years of the People's Republic, Jiang remained unpopular with many of Mao's CCP colleagues.

By the end of the 1950s some of those colleagues were questioning Mao Zedong's leadership. The "Three Bitter Years" weakened Mao's hold on power, for others in the CCP blamed him for China's economic troubles. Early in the 1960s, the top levels of the CCP were divided among factions struggling for power. Liu Shaoqi and Deng Xiaoping (a member of the CCP since the 1920s who had risen to a high rank within the party) took on more and more responsibility. Mao retreated—or was pushed—from active leadership into semiretirement. As far as the people of China were concerned, Mao was still the nation's figurehead, but he rarely appeared in public. The country was run by Liu, Deng, and others.

Mao did continue to speak out on foreign affairs. Since 1949, China had received both money and technical assistance—advisers, engineers, and equipment—from its ally the Soviet Union. But a split between the two nations developed in the late 1950s when Soviet premier Nikita Khrushchev began steering the Soviet Union toward slightly warmer relations with the United States.

Khrushchev, claimed Mao Zedong, had betrayed China. How could the head of the communist world talk about "peaceful coexistence" with the nation that supported the Nationalists and refused to recognize the People's Republic as the rightful government of China? Relations between the Soviet Union and China worsened when China attacked India in a border war and the Soviet Union, concerned that a Chinese victory might drag the superpowers into another world war, gave fighter planes to India.

Above all, Mao resented the fact that the Soviet Union, as the world's first communist state, expected to set policy for all other communists around the world. The Soviet Union and China formally ended relations in 1961, and for a time it seemed that the two nations might go to war. Rather than take orders from Moscow, Mao declared, China would replace the Soviet Union as the leader of world revolution.

Mao looked for new allies in the poorer nations of the world. He believed that the peasant villages of Africa, Southeast Asia, and South America would initiate a new wave of international socialism, just as China's countryside had been the birthplace of the Chinese revolution.

One ally lay just beyond China's southern border. Vietnam, like Korea, had been divided into two

Mao with Ho Chi Minh (right, with raised hat), the leader of the communist movement in North Vietnam. Mao found allies for China in Ho and other guerrilla and revolutionary leaders such as Fidel Castro of Cuba.

countries. A communist government had come to power in North Vietnam, next to China's Yunnan province, while the government of South Vietnam was supported by the United States. Almost immediately after Vietnam was divided in 1954, North and South Vietnam went to war. The United States aided the South and eventually entered the war against North Vietnam. At the same time, Mao's regime supplied aid to North Vietnam, although China never openly entered the war. So the Vietnam War, which dragged on for years, was not only tragic for Vietnam but was also a further cause of enmity between China and the United States.

During the early 1960s, Mao Zedong looked around him at what was happening in China and did not like what he saw. In Mao's opinion, too many people thought that the revolution had ended when the communists overthrew the Nationalists and founded the People's Republic. The passion and idealism of the early days had faded, and the revolutionaries had become comfortable office workers who were more concerned with the everyday business of their lives than with the ongoing battle of ideas and the unfolding process of history. But for Mao the revolution had no end. He liked to talk of the need for "constant struggle." And although he seemed to be quietly writing poetry and observing from the sidelines during the early 1960s, in reality he was preparing to throw China into its fiercest struggle yet.

C
H
A
P
T
E
R
7

THE REVOLUTION RETURNS

Once before, in the Jiangxi soviet in the early 1930s, Mao had lost much of his power. He had withdrawn into the shadows while others led the revolution. But he had not given up; he had simply bided his time and then, at the right moment, emerged to make himself more powerful than ever.

The same thing happened in the mid-1960s. By that time Liu Shaoqi, China's premier, had almost eclipsed Mao. Liu was considered Mao's successor as chairman of the CCP. A book written by Liu outsold Mao's writings. The title of the book was *How to Become a Good Communist*, but Mao considered Liu a bad communist. The only real voice of the Chinese Communist party, Mao believed, was Mao's. It was time for him to regain full control of the party and the country.

Mao was now in his early seventies. His health was poor. He suffered from bouts of pneumonia and was beginning to develop heart disease. His hands shook, he sometimes had difficulty walking, and he had begun to ramble incoherently when he spoke—signs of Parkinson's disease, which would worsen in the coming years. Yet his determination to shape China's destiny was as strong as ever.

Mao's chief ally in his return to power was Lin Baio, the commander of the People's Liberation Army. In 1964, Lin collected some of Mao's sayings into a little volume called *Quotations from Chairman Mao* and gave a copy to each PLA soldier. (Because the book was bound in red, it was sometimes called "the Little Red Book" outside China.) Lin told the army to become "a great school of Mao Zedong's thought."[1] The loyalty and support of the well-armed PLA lay firmly behind Mao Zedong. "Does the gun rule the party, or the party rule the gun?" Liu Shaoqi and others asked nervously. Soon it became clear that the gun—the army—ruled the party.

Mao had another formidable ally in his wife, Jiang Qing. She had long wanted to take part in government, and Mao now gave her a public role. Because she had been an actress, he put her in charge of the nation's cultural affairs. In this role she was of significant help to Mao when he unleashed a new wave of revolution on China, with the nation's cultural life as its starting point. But the Cultural Revolution reached far beyond literature and the arts. Its ultimate aim was nothing less than tearing down and rebuilding the fabric of Chinese society.

Mao launched the Cultural Revolution in 1966 with an appeal to young party members and students to return to the "pure" ideals of the revolution. Millions of young people, who had lived their whole lives in Mao Zedong's PRC, felt powerful and important when the chairman told them that China's future was in their hands. They answered his call with zeal. Organizing into semimilitary bands called Red Guards, they rampaged through universities, temples, and neighborhoods, painting slogans on walls and brandishing guns. Beijing University was the scene of some of the most passionate Red Guard activities. The university became "the battleground of vicious civil war among chaotic Red Guard factions, each claiming to represent Mao Zedong."[2]

The Red Guards declared war on "the Four Olds"—old ideas, old culture, old customs, and old habits. Their goal was to destroy everything that they considered traditional, religious, elitist, intellectual, or Western-leaning so that China's society and thought would become purely Chinese and purely communist. The Red Guards closed schools, turned temples and shrines into rubble, and burned hundreds of thousands of books. They accused professors, engineers, and doctors of being tools of the old class structure. "Better to be Red than to be an expert," the Red Guards would declare.

During the Cultural Revolution, people were beaten and humiliated for something as simple as wearing eyeglasses, which the Red Guards associated with weakness, intellectualism, snobbery, and West-

Brandishing Mao's "Little Red Book,"
young people flocked to join the Red Guards.
Soon they were waving rifles, not books, as the
Cultural Revolution engulfed China in a new
wave of violence.

ern influences. Quoting classical Chinese poetry, singing a song from a traditional Chinese opera, or reading a book translated from English was considered treachery to the revolution. Apparently the Red Guards did not know or did not care that Mao Zedong wore glasses, read and wrote traditional poetry, and had educated himself by reading Western books in translation.

Jiang Qing was the patron saint of the Red Guards. She encouraged their frenzies of destruction and reveled in the new power they gave her. Jiang and three of her closest supporters came to be called the Gang of Four. They often acted as Mao's mouthpieces, claiming to direct the Cultural Revolution in his name. Meanwhile, Mao was locked in a political struggle with Liu Shaoqi, Deng Xiaopeng, and others within the CCP who were appalled by the course the Cultural Revolution had taken. Mao denounced Liu and Deng for their willingness to depart from the ideals of pure socialism—for example, they recognized that collective farming was a failure and wanted to restore private ownership of land. Mao and Lin Baio gained the upper hand in the power struggle and promptly banished Liu and Deng from Beijing. Although Liu was technically still China's premier, he was kept a prisoner. He died in late 1969 when the insulin he needed to control his diabetes was withheld from him. Deng was placed under house arrest in Jiangxi province.

The Cultural Revolution tore China apart for several years. Hundreds of thousands of people were rounded up and sent to prison or to rural farms for "re-education," which often meant brainwashing or forced labor. In many regions fighting broke out between rival groups of Red Guards, or between the Red Guards and the army.

Admitting that things had gone too far, Mao tried to calm things down, urging the Red Guards to show restraint, but it proved much harder to put out the fire of the Cultural Revolution than it had been to ignite it. After practically running China for a few years, the Red Guards were unwilling to bow to authority—even to Mao's authority. In some areas Lin Baio had to call out the PLA to subdue the Red Guards. By the end of 1969, however, the worst excesses of the Cultural Revolution were dying down, and order was returning to China.

Lin Baio's close alliance with Mao had brought Lin considerable power and importance, which Mao viewed as a threat to his own position. Once the army had brought the Cultural Revolution under control, Mao clipped Lin's wings. He set about winning the support of the army commanders under Lin. When Lin realized what was happening, he accused Mao of being an old-fashioned emperor "under the skin of a Marxist." Said Lin, "Mao is a maniac of suspicion and persecution. . . . He can do no wrong for he makes others responsible for all the bad things."[3] Lin decided not to wait for prison or the labor camp. With his wife and son he fled Beijing in 1971. Official Chinese sources claimed that Lin had been involved in a plot to assassinate Mao. The truth of this claim will probably never be known, for Lin's plane went down over Mongolia. Everyone aboard died. The plane may have crashed, or it may have been shot down; details have never been made public. Either way, Mao's principal rival was dead.

Throughout the power struggles and the Cultural Revolution, Zhou Enlai had been a stabilizing influence, one whose loyalty to Mao and to the party was never questioned. Mao trusted the hard-working and capable Zhou, and Zhou used his gift of compromise to heal some of the rifts in the CCP. He became premier after Liu Shaoqi's death.

Mao's major criticism of Liu and Deng had been that they were "soft" on the United States. Ironically, the most important development in China in the years immediately following the Cultural Revolution was a warming of relations with the United States. Since 1949, Mao had been furious at the United States for keeping the PRC out of the United Nations. But during the 1960s several developments caused the United States to change its attitude toward the People's Republic.

One development was military. China tested its first nuclear bomb in 1964, and the United States realized that it could no longer ignore the existence of a country that had both nuclear weapons and one fifth of the world's population. The other development was economic. As long as the United States withheld diplomatic recognition from China, it could not do business with China—and American businesses were eager to open up trade with a nation of more than half a billion consumers.

In 1971 the United States withdrew its objection to the PRC's membership in the United Nations. China's seat was taken away from the Nationalist government in Taiwan and given to the People's Republic. The last barrier to improved relations fell when the United States announced that it was pulling out of the Vietnam War.

China's relationship with the United States entered a new phase in 1972 when, after much behind-the-scenes negotiation between Zhou Enlai and U.S. secretary of state Henry Kissinger, President Richard Nixon visited China. He was the first U.S. president ever to do so. Although formal diplomatic relations between China and the United States were not established until 1979, Nixon's visit paved the way for diplomatic recognition, cultural exchanges, trade agreements, and a surge of American tourists eager to see the country that had been off-limits to them for decades.

Nixon was photographed with a smiling Mao during the historic visit, but by that time Mao was seriously ill. Before each of his few public appearances, the chairman had to be dressed and medicated by nurses, and he was no longer able to carry on a long conversation. Zhou Enlai was running the country with Mao's endorsement. In 1973, Zhou brought Deng Xiaoping back to Beijing to help him, and gradually Deng took on responsibility for China's economy.

The elderly and ailing Mao greets U.S. president Richard Nixon on Nixon's visit to China in 1972. The visit marked the beginning of warmer relations between the two nations.

In 1975, Zhou announced that China would embark on an economic program called the Four Modernizations (of farming, industry, defense, and science). Some of Zhou's new policies departed from socialist doctrine—for example, farm workers were now allowed to cultivate private gardens and sell their produce for private profit in free markets. Factions sprang up in support of or in opposition to these new policies. The opposition was led by Jiang Qing's Gang of Four. A more moderate group led by Deng supported Zhou. Deng's power was on the rise. Zhou was dying; he had been battling cancer for years. It seemed clear that Deng Xiaoping would succeed Zhou Enlai as China's leader.

Mao was on his sickbed, but, seeing Deng's popularity increase, he mustered enough energy to arrange yet another of his dramatic reversals. He allowed the Gang of Four to begin spreading propaganda critical of Deng. (Some historians feel that by this time Jiang Qing dominated the gravely ill chairman, carrying out her own wishes while claiming that they were Mao's orders.) Many people in China, remembering the dire years of the Cultural Revolution, were displeased to see Jiang Qing returning to power. When Zhou Enlai died in January 1976, a mourning ceremony for him in Tiananmen Square in Beijing turned into a mass demonstration against the Gang of Four. Mao used the outbreak in Tiananmen Square as an excuse to get rid of Deng Xiaoping. Blaming Deng for the demonstration, he stripped Deng of his position and made Hua Guofeng, a relatively insignificant party member from Hunan, China's new premier.

Zhou Enlai was not the only veteran of the Long March and the revolution to die in 1976. Zhu De, Mao's old comrade-in-arms, died in July. And Mao Zedong himself was dying. He was bedridden and needed round-the-clock medical care; he could breathe only with the help of a respirator. The end of his "constant struggle" came on September 9, when he died at the age of eighty-two.

MAO'S
8 LEGACY

Mao Zedong's most fervent hope was that Maoism would live on for centuries and that China would stay on the course he had set. Yet after Mao's death, the fate of the Chinese Communist party—and of China—was beyond his control.

Throughout the long decline of Mao's health, his friends and enemies had wondered what would happen and who would rule China when he died. The members of the Politburo—the Central Committee of the CCP—had maneuvered to secure their future positions even as Mao lay dying. "The breath had hardly left Mao's shrunken lungs when the Politburo went into session, wrangling over the corpse and the legacy," says Harrison Salisbury, a specialist in modern Chinese history.[1]

After Mao's death, Deng's supporters came to the fore. In October 1976 they ordered the arrest of the Gang of Four for a variety of crimes, including disobedience to the CCP. The Gang of Four stood trial in 1980–1981. All four were sentenced to life imprisonment. In 1991 the Chinese government announced that Jiang Qing had committed suicide in prison.

During 1977, Deng gradually took over from Hua Guofeng, who faded into the background of Chinese politics. Deng Xiaoping became what Mao Zedong had once been: the most powerful man in China. A number of other party leaders moved into and out of the top official positions in China, but Deng was always firmly in charge, whether he was in office or ruling from behind the scenes.

Deng steered China on a tricky course: He wanted to introduce greater economic freedom without giving the people more political or social freedom. He discovered, however, that it is not possible to change the way people work and do business without having some other changes creep into society. For example, to attract investments and industrial development, Deng opened China up to business with Western nations, including the United States. American companies began doing business in China. Inevitably, the Chinese people had more contact with Westerners, and they began adopting some Western habits. People stopped wearing the once-universal blue "Mao jacket"; men and women began wearing blue jeans and miniskirts on the streets of Shanghai and other cities. The radios and cassette players churned out by China's new factories played the music of Madonna and U2 instead of CCP anthems.

Deng Xiaoping reviews troops in Beijing, 1984. Upon Mao's death, Deng seized the reins of power and steered China toward moderate economic reforms.

Some people in China began to think that the new openness and freedom should go beyond fashion to ideas and politics. A movement developed to introduce Western-style democracy to China, where since 1949 the CCP had permitted no challenges to its rule. The pro-democracy movement was especially strong among young people and students, some of whom began openly criticizing Deng and other CCP figures. Observers wondered how long the Chinese government, one of the most repressive in the world, would tolerate dissent.

The answer came in June 1989, when thousands of students and workers in Beijing and elsewhere defied government orders and demanded democratic reforms. A huge crowd of demonstrators gathered in Tiananmen Square. To the shock of people around the world, the government ordered PLA troops and tanks into Tiananmen Square to "restrain" the unarmed protestors. Hundreds were killed; thousands more were arrested or fled the country. The CCP had made it brutally clear that no dissent from the official party line would be tolerated in China, no matter how liberal the nation's economic life had become.

F*orty years after Mao proclaimed the birth of the "new China" in Tiananmen Square, his portrait was spattered with paint by protestors who gathered in the square to demand democratic reforms. Their protest was ruthlessly crushed; the totalitarianism of Mao's rule lingers on in China.*

In 1992 the Soviet Union disintegrated into a dozen independent states. Communism, which had reigned in the Soviet Union for most of the twentieth century, lost its hold on Russia and became just one of many competing economic and political philosophies. The world's first communist state had ceased to exist—leaving China the only large communist nation in the world. China's government stood alone in political isolation, clinging to a system that had been overthrown or discredited elsewhere.

The years before Mao's death were filled with speculation about his successor and about the fate of China after his passing. The same is true of Deng. As Deng's health declined, people in China and elsewhere wondered whether any of the party's other leaders would be strong enough to take and hold supreme power on Deng's death. Many believed that Deng's passing might trigger sweeping changes in China's political landscape. Of the nation's 1.2 billion people, about 55 million are said to be members of the CCP, but many branches of the party have all but ceased to function, and the pro-democracy movement is still alive.

In January 1995, Deng Xiaoping's daughter reported that her ninety-year-old father was seriously ill. Like Mao, Deng hopes that the one-party socialist state for which he fought will remain stable after his death. He has groomed CCP officials to carry on after him—but he knows that China's future may be determined by others. "As long as we, the older generation, are still around, the hostile forces know that change cannot happen," he said in 1993. "But who can guarantee this once we old men pass away?"[2]

Mao's status in China changed in the years after his death. The cultlike worship of Chairman Mao ended when Deng Xiaoping publicly criticized some of Mao's actions. Shortly after Mao's death, Deng said that "there would be no New China without Chairman Mao"—but he added that Mao was a fallible human leader, not a god. Deng and other CCP spokespersons also began emphasizing the contributions of others, such as Zhou Enlai and Zhu De.

Historian Ross Terrill wrote in 1980: "Deng Xiaoping, driving force of the Chinese government, has said that Mao was 70 percent good and 30 percent bad. In private the judgment is harsher; many Chinese resent, despise, or hate Mao."[3] Yet there are many who feel that their lives have been better in the People's Republic than they would have been in the old China, the China of the downtrodden peasant.

Mao Zedong's actions are now part of history—indeed, he *made* history for one fifth of the world's people. Yet Mao himself is ultimately unknowable. Some world leaders have left documents that give us a view into their inner lives. But Mao's poetry is stately and formal, filled with allusions to historical events, not personal revelations. And if he ever revealed his deepest thoughts or questioned his soul in letters or journals, those documents have been destroyed or buried in party archives. Mao and his followers and successors edited his life just as they edited the novels that Mao had loved so much as a young man. He carefully presented only what he wanted people to know about him, and in the end there is little by which to measure him but his deeds. Mao the man looms large but blankly impenetrable, like the enormous portrait of him that still hangs in Tiananmen Square.

Mao has been viewed as both a hero and a tyrant. His patriotism is undeniable; he fought valiantly to defend China against the Japanese, and he would undoubtedly have gone to war to protect his country from any other aggressor. He was a visionary who dreamed of a new China and had the force of will to reshape the world to fit his dream. Yet visionaries are dangerous. Sometimes they cannot tolerate the existence of anything or anyone outside their own narrow field of vision. Mao Zedong was an idealist who gave the Chinese people freedoms they had never known. He was also a tyrant, who ruthlessly crushed anyone who dared to dream of freedoms beyond those he offered. He may be both a savior and a villain, but one thing is certain: In shaping the lives of one fifth of the world's population, Mao Zedong had a greater impact on the destiny of the Chinese people than any other single person, except perhaps the emperor who first united China 2,200 years ago.

CHRONOLOGY

1644   Manchus from the northeast invade China and establish the Qing dynasty.

1839–   The First Opium War; China is defeated by Great
1842   Britain and forced to open ports to foreign trade.

1851–   The Taiping Rebellion, a peasant revolt against the
1864   Manchus; 20 million die before the revolt is crushed by imperial forces.

1856–   The Second Opium War; China is defeated by Great
1860   Britain and France; foreign control of the Chinese empire increases.

1893   Mao Zedong is born in Shaoshan, Hunan province, December 26.

1899–   Nationalist societies launch the Boxer Rebellion
1900   against foreign interference; the rebellion is ended by foreign forces.

1912   Nationalists end the Qing dynasty; the Republic of China is founded.

1916   The republic breaks up; warlords and the National-
        ist party struggle for supremacy.

1918   Mao graduates from school in Hunan, goes to
        Beijing.

1919   May Fourth Movement.

1920   Mao leads socialist group in Hunan; marries Yang
        Kaihui.

1921   Chinese Communist party (CCP) is organized; Mao
        is named Hunan secretary.

1927   Mao calls for rural peasant revolution; Nationalists
        and communists go to war; Mao retreats to Well
        Mountain.

1930   Mao's wife and sister are executed by Nationalist
        forces; Mao marries He Zizhen.

1931   Japan invades and occupies Manchuria (northeast-
        ern China).

1934–   The Long March; Mao and other communists travel
1935   north to new stronghold in northwest China.

1937   Japan invades China. Nationalists and communists
        fight the Japanese.

1945   Japan withdraws from China.

1946–   Communists and Nationalists fight for control of
1949   China.

1949   Nationalists flee to Taiwan. Victorious communists
        establish People's Republic of China, with Mao as
        chairman of the CCP; Mao visits Moscow.

1950   China enters Korean War and also invades Tibet.

1958   Mao announces Five-Year Plan to make the "Great
        Leap Forward."

1960–
1963   China experiences widespread famine and economic troubles.

1966   Mao encourages young CCP members to launch the Cultural Revolution.

1971   The People's Republic is given China's seat in the United Nations.

1972   U.S. president Richard Nixon visits China.

1976   Mao Zedong dies on September 9, at the age of 82.

1977   Deng Xiaoping becomes China's new leader.

1989   Protestors demanding democratic reforms are quelled by government forces in Tiananmen Square, Beijing.

N O T E S

CHAPTER ONE

1. Quoted in Harrison E. Salisbury, *The New Emperors: China in the Era of Mao and Deng*, New York: Avon, 1993, p. 26.
2. Quoted in Edgar Snow, *Red Star over China*, New York: Grove, 1968, p. 133.
3. Quoted in Ross Terrill, *Mao: A Biography*, New York: Harper, 1980, p. 8.
4. Quoted in Snow, p. 131.
5. Quoted in Snow, p. 133.
6. Quoted in Snow, p. 132.
7. Quoted in Snow, p. 133.
8. Quoted in Terrill, p. 11.
9. Quoted in Snow, p. 135.
10. Quoted in Snow, p. 136.

CHAPTER TWO

1. Quoted in Edgar Snow, *Red Star over China*, New York: Grove, 1968, p. 136.
2. Quoted in Snow, p. 136.

CHAPTER THREE

1. Ross Terrill, *Mao: A Biography*, New York: Harper, 1980, p. 21.
2. Quoted in Edgar Snow, *Red Star over China*, New York: Grove, 1968, p. 143.
3. Terrill, p. 27.
4. Terrill, p. 33.
5. Terrill, p. 34.
6. Terrill, p. 36.
7. Snow, p. 151.
8. Snow, p. 152.
9. Terrill, pp.43–44.
10. Terrill, p. 49.
11. Terrill, p. 79.
12. Terrill, p. 81.
13. Terrill, p. 83.
14. Quoted in Peter Carter, *Mao*, New York: New American Library, 1980, p. 67.

CHAPTER FOUR

1. Peter Carter, *Mao*, New York: New American Library, 1980, p. 72.
2. Quoted in Ross Terrill, *Mao: A Biography*, New York: Harper, 1980, p. 129.
3. Carter, p. 97.

CHAPTER FIVE

1. Ross Terrill, *Mao: A Biography*, New York: Harper, 1980, p. 163.
2. Eric Chou, *Mao Tse-tung: The Man and the Myth*, New York: Stein and Day, 1982, p. 157.
3. Quoted in Terrill, p. 144.
4. Peter Carter, *Mao*, New York: New American Library, 1980, p. 118.

5. Quoted in Terrill, p. 183.
6. Terrill, p. 151.
7. Quoted in Terrill, p. 199.

CHAPTER SIX

1. Ross Terrill, *Mao: A Biography*, New York: Harper, 1980, p. 212.
2. Terrill, p. 212.
3. Eric Chou, *Mao Tse-tung: The Man and the Myth*, New York: Stein and Day, 1982, p. 172.
4. Chou, p. 184.
5. Chou, p. 190.
6. Chou, p. 245.

CHAPTER SEVEN

1. Quoted in Ross Terrill, *Mao: A Biography*, New York: Harper, 1980, p. 306.
2. Harrison Salisbury, *The New Emperors: China in the Era of Mao and Deng*, New York: Avon, 1993, p. 320.
3. Quoted in Eric Chou, *Mao Tse-tung: The Man and the Myth*, New York: Stein and Day, 1982, p. 237–238.

CHAPTER EIGHT

1. Harrison Salisbury, *The New Emperors: China in the Era of Mao and Deng*, New York: Avon, 1993, p. 370.
2. Russell Watson, "The Last Days of a Dynasty?" *Newsweek*, January 30, 1995, p. 40.
3. Ross Terrill, *Mao: A Biography*, New York: Harper, 1980, p. 433.

B I B L I O G R A P H Y

Books for young adults are marked with an asterisk (*).

Barnett, A. Doak. *China After Mao*. Princeton, N.J.: Princeton University Press, 1967.

Bloodworth, Dennis. *The Messiah and the Mandarins: Mao Tsetung and the Ironies of Power*. New York: Atheneum, 1982.

Bouc, Alain. *Mao Tse-tung: A Guide to His Thought*. Translated by Paul Auster and Lydia Davis. New York: St. Martin's Press, 1977.

Carter, Peter. *Mao*. New York: New American Library, 1980.

Chen, Jerome. *Mao and the Chinese Revolution*. New York: Oxford University Press, 1965.

Chou, Eric. *Mao Tse-tung: The Man and the Myth*. New York: Stein and Day, 1982.

*Dunster, Jack. *China and Mao Zedong*. Minneapolis: Lerner Publications and Cambridge University Press, 1983.

*Fritz, Jean. *China's Long March: 6,000 Miles of Danger*. New York: Putnam's, 1988.

*Garza, Hedda. *Mao Zedong*. New York: Chelsea House, 1988.

*Hoobler, Dorothy, and Thomas. *U.S.-China Relations Since World War II*. New York: Franklin Watts, 1981.

Howard, Roger. *Mao Tse-tung and the Chinese People*. New York: Monthly Review Press, 1977.

Karnow, Stanley. *Mao and China: From Revolution to Revolution*. New York: Viking, 1976.

_____. *Mao and China: A Legacy of Turmoil*. 3d edition. New York: Viking, 1990.

*Kurland, Gerald. *Mao Tse-tung: Founder of Communist China*. Charlotteville, N.Y.: SamHar Press, 1972.

Lawrance, Alan. *Mao Zedong: A Biography*. Westport, Conn.: Greenwood Press, 1991.

Lifton, Robert J. *Revolutionary Immortality: Mao Tse-tung and the Chinese Cultural Revolution*. New York: Random House, 1968.

Mao Tsetung. *Quotations from Chairman Mao*. Edited and introduced by Stuart R. Schram. New York: Bantam, 1967.

*Marrin, Albert. *Mao Tse-tung and His China*. New York: Viking Children's Books, 1989.

*Painter, Desmond. *Mao Tse-tung*. San Diego: Greenhaven Press, 1980.

Payne, Robert. *Mao Tse-tung*. New York: Weybright and Talley, 1969.

*Poole, Frederick King. *Mao Zedong*. New York: Franklin Watts, 1982.

Rice, Edward E. *Mao's Way*. Berkeley: University of California Press, 1972.

*Roberson, John R. *China from Manchu to Mao (1699–1976)*. New York: Atheneum, 1980.

Salisbury, Harrison E. *The New Emperors: China in the Era of Mao and Deng*. New York: Avon, 1993.

Schram, Stuart R. *Mao Tse-tung*. New York: Simon & Schuster, 1966.

_____. *Mao Zedong: A Preliminary Reassessment*. New York: St. Martin's Press, 1983.

Snow, Edgar. *Red Star over China*. New York: Grove, 1968. Originally published 1937.

Solomon, Richard H. *Mao's Revolution and the Chinese Political Culture*. Berkeley: University of California Press, 1971.

*Stefoff, Rebecca. *China*. New York: Chelsea House, 1991.

Suyin, Han. *Wind in the Tower: Mao Tsetung and the Chinese Revolution*. Boston: Little, Brown, 1976.

Terrill, Ross. *Mao: A Biography*. New York: Harper, 1980.

*Warner, Dennis A. *Hurricane from China*. New York: Macmillan, 1961.

Wilson, Dick. *Mao, The People's Emperor*. New York: Doubleday, 1980.

INDEX